PRESENTED TO

FROM

ON

THE ONE YEAR®
INSPIRATIONAL WORDS OF JESUS
FOR WOMEN

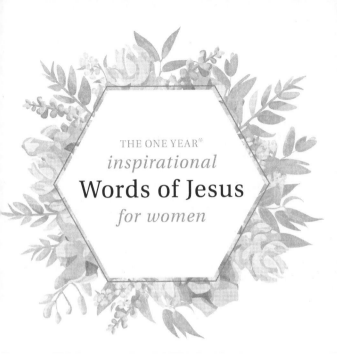

THE ONE YEAR®
inspirational
Words of Jesus
for women

Robin Merrill

TYNDALE
MOMENTUM®

The nonfiction imprint of
Tyndale House Publishers, Inc.

Visit Tyndale online at www.tyndale.com.

Visit Tyndale Momentum online at www.tyndalemomentum.com.

TYNDALE, Tyndale Momentum, and Tyndale's quill logo are registered trademarks of Tyndale House Publishers, Inc. The Tyndale Momentum logo is a trademark of Tyndale House Publishers, Inc. Tyndale Momentum is the nonfiction imprint of Tyndale House Publishers, Inc., Carol Stream, Illinois.

The One Year Inspirational Words of Jesus for Women

Produced with the assistance of Hudson Bible (www.HudsonBible.com). Project staff includes Christopher D. Hudson, Len Woods, and Mary Larsen.

Cover illustration of floral design copyright © bugega/iStockphoto. All rights reserved.

Designed by Eva M. Winters

Edited by Deborah King

Published in association with the literary agency of The Steve Laube Agency

Scripture quotations are taken from the *Holy Bible*, New Living Translation, copyright © 1996, 2004, 2015 by Tyndale House Foundation. Used by permission of Tyndale House Publishers, Inc., Carol Stream, Illinois 60188. All rights reserved.

For information about special discounts for bulk purchases, please contact Tyndale House Publishers at csresponse@tyndale.com, or call 1-800-323-9400.

ISBN 978-1-4964-2304-7

Printed in China

24   23   22   21   20   19   18
 7   6   5   4   3   2   1

INTRODUCTION

WRITING THIS BOOK gave me a special opportunity to dig in to the words of Jesus. I thought I already knew them. I thought I knew what I wanted to say about them. But the more time I spent with them, the more they spoke to me—the more *Jesus* spoke to me through those red letters, and I realized that yes, I do know him, but oh, how I want to know him more.

It would be difficult to encounter the Jesus of the Bible and not change. In fact, when I revisit a verse I think I know well, I find it changing me *again*. Because the Word of God is alive and active. And love and light and life are packed into each of the words that Jesus spoke.

It would have been so exciting to be Nicodemus, to seek wisdom from Wisdom himself in the cool of the night. Or to be the Samaritan woman at the well, meeting the Messiah in the heat of noon. But we, too, get to encounter

Jesus, as often as we want, through his recorded words, and they are every bit as powerful now as they were when he spoke them aloud. Because the Bible is timeless. Jesus is timeless. His teachings, his promises, his grace—all still 100 percent valid today.

We have collected his most inspirational statements here for you. It is my prayer that, as you interact with these verses, they may change you and then change you again, that they may comfort you, encourage you, and inspire you—but most of all, that they may leave you wanting more of Jesus.

Robin Merrill

BECOMING HUMBLE

God blesses those who are humble,
for they will inherit the whole earth.

MATTHEW 5:5

HUMILITY is one of the marks of following Jesus. Jesus says we will inherit the earth if we show humility, a special kind of teachability—so it must be pretty important. But many of us begin our quest for humility by trying to control our behavior, which just doesn't work.

Humility is a condition of the heart. Our hearts change as we spend time gazing on the greatness of God. When we read his Word, we see our own sin in comparison with his righteousness. When we talk to him, we remember that he is wise and we are foolish. As our hearts change, our outward attitudes and behaviors follow. When we spend time with God, we can't help but become more humble.

True intimacy with God always brings humility.
BETH MOORE

PURE HEARTS

*God blesses those whose hearts are
pure, for they will see God.*

MATTHEW 5:8

ONLY THOSE WITH pure hearts can see God. If we are
harboring some ill will or hiding some sin or refusing to
give some part of ourselves to God, we can look for him
all we want, but we won't see him. As we come before
God, we must rid our hearts of anything that might come
between him and us.

It can feel excruciating and almost impossible to let
go of our treasured sins sometimes. But when we do catch
that glimpse of God, we'll realize that everything we've
given up pales in comparison to seeing him.

*It is a pleasant thing to behold the light, but sore eyes
are not able to look upon it; the pure in heart shall
see God, but the defiled in conscience shall rather
choose to be buried under rocks and mountains
than to behold the presence of the Lamb.*

ANNE BRADSTREET

LOVE YOUR ENEMY

Love your enemies!
Pray for those who persecute you!

MATTHEW 5:44

TO LOVE AN ENEMY seems an unfathomably tall order. Praying for someone who has harmed us—and may still have plans to harm us—would be impossible if it weren't for the power of Jesus.

Jesus would not give us an order without enabling us to follow it. But we must seek him for strength, wisdom, and courage to obey. As we pray for people who wish to harm us, he will reach into our hearts and change us. When we truly seek Jesus in prayer, love is the only possible result.

It is not on our forgiveness any more than on our goodness that the world's healing hinges, but on His. When He tells us to love our enemies, He gives, along with the command, the love itself.

CORRIE TEN BOOM

PRIVATE PRAYER

*When you pray, go away by yourself, shut the door
behind you, and pray to your Father in private. Then
your Father, who sees everything, will reward you.*

MATTHEW 6:6

WOMEN LEAD BUSY LIVES. It may be tempting to think
we pray enough in church or before meals. But while
these public opportunities for prayer can be good, Jesus
tells us that we need to also carve out some alone time
with God.

Choose a place to meet with God regularly. It could
be in a cozy chair at home, or it might be in your car just
before you go in to work. It doesn't matter the location
so much as the state of your heart. Create some time and
space for your heart to be alone with God. Then he will
reward you.

*Build yourself a cell in your heart
and retire there to pray.*
CATHERINE OF SIENA

IT'S NOT MAGIC

When you pray, don't babble on and on as the Gentiles do. They think their prayers are answered merely by repeating their words again and again.

MATTHEW 6:7

SOMETIMES WE APPROACH prayer nervously because we think of it as a magic spell that we might mess up. But Jesus frees us from the lie that if we don't pray long enough or say the words just right, God may not answer.

When you pray, you are kneeling before the throne of God. So don't worry about following a certain formula for prayer. God is not a genie or a fairy who will answer the way we want if we say the words just right. He is our loving father, and he already knows our heart's needs and desires. Simply open yourself to him, and don't focus on "doing it right." If your heart is right, you can't do prayer wrong.

Prayer is the application of the heart to God, and the internal exercise of love.

JEANNE-MARIE GUYON

A DAILY DISCIPLINE

Give us today the food we need.

MATTHEW 6:11

AS JESUS WAS TEACHING his disciples how to pray, he stressed our need for daily reliance on God. He did not say, "Give us the food we'll need till next Sunday" or "Give us enough food to last until we think to pray again." Jesus' request for daily food showed the disciples (and all his followers) that prayer—and trusting God to provide for our everyday needs—should be a daily discipline.

We don't have to wait till we're in the foxhole to call out to God. We can pray to him all day long, every day, all year. In giving his life, Jesus made such direct, immediate access to God possible. We can take advantage of this access anytime.

Is prayer your steering wheel or your spare tire?

CORRIE TEN BOOM

THE FATHER OF LIES

[The devil] has always hated the truth, because there is no truth in him. When he lies, it is consistent with his character; for he is a liar and the father of lies.

JOHN 8:44

THE PHARISEES DIDN'T believe in Jesus, because they trusted that their ancestry as children of Abraham was enough to save them. But this was a lie from Satan to keep them from God's truth. What lies have you believed? Jesus' words can encourage us with this truth: the lies that we're battling against every day come from the enemy.

We don't serve the father of lies. We serve the God of truth. We don't have to believe these lies when they're fired at us. We can reject them in the name of Jesus, in the name of his love.

We're going to have to let truth scream louder to our souls than the lies that have infected us.

BETH MOORE

A PRIVATE MATTER

When you fast, comb your hair and wash your face.
Then no one will notice that you are fasting, except
your Father, who knows what you do in private. And
your Father, who sees everything, will reward you.

MATTHEW 6:17-18

FASTING—abstaining from such things as food, social media, or electronics—should be carried out with humility. If we show the world how miserable our devotion makes us, how can that bring glory to God?

Fasting is a private matter between God and us. And when we are discreet about it and use it to truly seek God, he will reward us. That's not to say we fast in order to earn a reward; we fast in order to seek and worship God.

Do you not know that fasting can master
concupiscence, lift up the soul, confirm it in the paths
of virtue, and prepare a fine reward for the Christian?

HEDWIG OF SILESIA

CHOOSE GOD, AND BE FREE

*No one can serve two masters.... You cannot
serve God and be enslaved to money.*

MATTHEW 6:24

JESUS WARNED US that it's impossible to serve God if we place our trust in money. When we trust money, it enslaves us—it consumes us and sucks out our energy, joy, and peace. When we choose to trust only in God, those shackles fall off.

Most of us, at some point, worry about finances or seek to gain more money because of the sense of security we think it will provide. But money can't provide peace or joy. Only God can do that. So let's choose to serve only him today.

*My very soul was flooded with a celestial light.... For
the first time I realized that I had been trying to hold
the world in one hand and the Lord in the other.*

FANNY J. CROSBY

GOD WILL PROVIDE

*Don't worry about these things, saying, "What will
we eat? What will we drink? What will we wear?" . . .
Your heavenly Father already knows all your needs.*

MATTHEW 6:31-32

WOMEN FREQUENTLY feel a burden to plan ahead. We often manage the household and decide how to best care for our families. But if this leads us to worry about tomorrow, then we are wasting our precious energy. Jesus tells us that God already knows what we need, and he will provide. He will make sure we—and our loved ones—are fed, clothed, and cared for.

We don't need to feel anxious about these details. We just need to trust God and then rest in his provision.

*I have started houses with no more than the
price of a loaf of bread and prayers, for with
Him who comforts me, I can do anything.*

FRANCES XAVIER CABRINI

THE STANDARD YOU USE

The standard you use in judging is the
standard by which you will be judged.

MATTHEW 7:2

WE CHRISTIANS can be excellent judgers. Jesus warned us long ago that we should be careful about judging others, because we will be judged by the same standard. For example, I might get frustrated with a sister who carouses on the weekends, but what are my vices? I might be ready to ridicule my brother who exaggerates so often, but what white lies did I tell this week? And that child who is so rude? Am I rude right back?

Let's show grace to others. Who knows what circumstances lie behind their behavior?

Incline us O God! to think humbly of ourselves, to be
severe only in the examination of our own conduct,
to consider our fellow-creatures with kindness, and
to judge of all they say and do with that charity
which we would desire from them ourselves.

JANE AUSTEN

SAVE YOUR ENERGY

*First get rid of the log in your own eye;
then you will see well enough to deal
with the speck in your friend's eye.*

MATTHEW 7:5

JUDGING OTHERS can make us feel smugly good for a few
fleeting moments. But it's exhausting. The enemy wants
us to stay focused on others' sin so we deplete the energy
needed to accomplish things that matter and so we ignore
the sin in our own hearts.

Jesus is asking us to invest our energy in actions and
attitudes that lead to true joy: serving, loving, and listening to others. If we focus on cleansing our own hearts—
rather than on the faults of others—we'll be able to love
others the way God does.

If you judge people, you have no time to love them.

MOTHER TERESA

SEEK AND FIND

Keep on seeking, and you will find.
MATTHEW 7:7

ONE OF JESUS' SWEETEST promises is that if you seek God, you will find him. When we really want to know God, he makes himself available to us. When we truly open our hearts to his love, he pours it into us until we are overflowing.

Seek God in his Word. Seek him in prayer. Seek him in creation. Seek him in others. Seek him in worship. Seek him in praise and thanksgiving. Seek him in service. Seeking God is never wasted effort. Even if the rewards are not immediate, they are forthcoming. There is no such thing as seeking God in vain.

I sought him whom my Soul did Love,
With tears I sought him earnestly;
He bow'd his ear down from Above,
In vain I did not seek or cry.
ANNE BRADSTREET

GOOD GIFTS

If you sinful people know how to give good gifts to your children, how much more will your heavenly Father give good gifts to those who ask him.

MATTHEW 7:11

GOD IS OUR FATHER. And in the same way that we want to provide plentifully for our children, he wants to take care of us. All we have to do is ask.

Ask God to meet your basic needs. Ask him to show you ways you can serve others and glorify him. Ask him to fulfill your wildest dreams. Ask him to show you dreams you haven't even imagined yet. Ask him to wrap his arms around you. Ask him to reveal himself to you, so that you may know him more fully and live more richly.

No honest prayer goes unheard.

God's gifts put man's best dreams to shame.
ELIZABETH BARRETT BROWNING

A SINGLE SPARROW

*What is the price of two sparrows—one copper
coin? But not a single sparrow can fall to the
ground without your Father knowing it.*

MATTHEW 10:29

GOD KNOWS the tiniest sparrow. He knows her mind and
her heart. He created her. God provides for the sparrow.
He knows her path. He knows where she flies and when
she falls.

You are so much more valuable to God than a sparrow. So often we feel as if we are alone in this world.
We struggle with feelings of self-doubt. We struggle to
make ends meet. But we don't have to struggle. We can
trust God, who knows our minds, our hearts, our paths.
He created you, and he knows your needs. You are his
beloved.

*Each little flower that opens,
each little bird that sings,
He made their glowing colors,
He made their tiny wings.*

CECIL FRANCES ALEXANDER

TAKE COURAGE

Don't be afraid. . . . Take courage. I am here!

MATTHEW 14:27

JESUS SENT HIS DISCIPLES out in a boat while he went off alone to pray. While they sailed in the middle of the night, the disciples faced fierce winds and waves that battered the boat. When Jesus walked out on the water toward them in the middle of the storm, they thought they saw an apparition and became terrified. But Jesus said, "Take courage. I am here!" Jesus was there with them. And he is here with us (see Matthew 28:20).

There will be storms in this life, times when we are anxious and afraid. During these times, we can call out to Jesus in prayer. We can hear his voice through his Word, and we can take courage.

Courage doesn't mean you don't get afraid.
Courage means you don't let fear stop you.

BETHANY HAMILTON

GOOD NEWS

The Son of Man will come with his angels
in the glory of his Father and will judge
all people according to their deeds.

MATTHEW 16:27

JESUS WILL RETURN to earth to "judge all people." There are several ways to receive this news. We can tremble in fear at this daunting fact. Or we can allow it to spur us into action: to follow Christ with our whole heart. If we are living every moment in humble service to him, we can look forward to his return with joy and anticipation—and without any fear.

We don't know when he is coming back—only that he is. And whether it happens generations from now or tomorrow, his return is good news for those who belong to him.

I wish He would come in my lifetime so that
I could take off my crown and lay it at His feet.

QUEEN VICTORIA

SEVENTY TIMES SEVEN

[Peter] asked, "Lord, how often should I forgive
someone who sins against me? Seven times?"
"No, not seven times," Jesus replied,
"but seventy times seven!"

MATTHEW 18:21-22

PETER THOUGHT forgiving others seven times was generous. But Jesus teaches us that our forgiveness of others'
wrongs should be limitless. We can't hold others' sin over
them.

We have all done wrong, and we are all in need of forgiveness. So, if a brother or sister has offended you, don't
think that the relationship is beyond repair. Go to him
or her, share your heart, and if he or she repents, extend
forgiveness freely. It could be the birth, or the rebirth, of
an amazing friendship.

O Lord God . . . though our sins be seven, though
our sins be seventy times seven, though our sins
be more in number than the hairs of our head, yet
give us grace in loving penitence to cast ourselves
down into the depths of Thy compassion.

CHRISTINA ROSSETTI

NOTHING IS IMPOSSIBLE

You don't have enough faith. . . . I tell you the truth, if you had faith even as small as a mustard seed, you could say to this mountain, "Move from here to there," and it would move. Nothing would be impossible.

MATTHEW 17:20

IF YOU'VE EVER FELT God calling you to something big, you've likely heard voices telling you that it just isn't possible. Or maybe you've doubted that your idea would ever become a reality due to various obstacles. Don't give up hope, because with God, nothing is impossible. Jesus says so. Every missions trip, every orphanage, every food drive started out as a dream in the heart of someone who believed in a big, powerful God.

So let yourself dream big and pursue those dreams. Ask God to guide you. Then hang on for the ride. It will likely take you places you haven't yet dreamed of.

God raises the level of the impossible.

CORRIE TEN BOOM

EVERY MINUTE MATTERS

You also must be ready all the time, for the
Son of Man will come when least expected.

MATTHEW 24:44

THESE WORDS FROM Jesus are like the locker room pep talk, when the coach says, "Play the whole game like you're in overtime." Jesus wants us to live on our toes. We're to live soberly, attentively, intentionally, and expectantly, as if each minute matters—because it does.

This isn't to say that we can never relax. But even when we are resting, we are to confidently rest in the knowledge that Jesus could appear at any second. And when he does appear, don't you want to be able to fall to your knees and say, "Savior! I'm ready for what comes next!"

Only faintly now I see Him,
With the darkened veil between,
But a blessed day is coming,
When His glory shall be seen.

CARRIE E. BRECK

GOD'S WILL BE DONE

*Don't you realize that I could ask my Father for
thousands of angels to protect us, and he would send
them instantly? But if I did, how would the Scriptures
be fulfilled that describe what must happen now?*

MATTHEW 26:53-54

WHEN THE ARMED crowd arrested Jesus, Peter leaped into
action and cut off the ear of the high priest's slave. Jesus
promptly told Peter to put his sword away, saying, "Don't
you understand who I am? I could easily choose to avoid
arrest, but that's not God's plan!" Jesus trusted God, even
when it meant his own death.

It's often difficult to trust God's will for our lives, but
trusting him is the only way to stay within the safety of
that will. We mustn't try to fight against God's perfect
plan. He is in control. He always has been, and he's never
let us down before.

Leave results to God.

ELIZABETH BARRETT BROWNING

THE GREAT COMMISSION

Go and make disciples of all the nations,
baptizing them in the name of the Father
and the Son and the Holy Spirit.

MATTHEW 28:19

HERE'S A CHALLENGE straight from the lips of Jesus. As Jesus' followers, we are commanded to make other followers. This doesn't mean every Christian needs to move to another country, learn a new language, and navigate a new culture. If we all pack up and leave home, who will share Jesus with the people in our own neighborhoods and communities?

Missions isn't just about faraway lands. It's about *all* lands. All people need Jesus. That includes the people you work with, the people you live near, and the people who live in your home.

Make the blessed Savior known,
Till all hearts shall be His throne;
Till He rules the world alone,
Make Him known.

CARRIE E. BRECK & HELEN ALEXANDER

THE BEGINNING

*Repent of your sins and turn to God, for
the Kingdom of Heaven is near.*

MATTHEW 4:17

THESE WORDS OF JESUS mark the beginning of his earthly ministry. How appropriate that this journey begins with the command to repent. Because don't all our journeys with Jesus begin with repentance? Doesn't every breakthrough, every miracle, every spiritual growth spurt begin with us falling on our knees and saying, "I'm sorry, Jesus"?

Is there anything keeping you from journeying further with Jesus right now? Is there anything that you can repent of, so that you can keep going and growing?

*Here's the deal, y'all. God. Already. Knows. His people
are a hot, sinful mess, so when we simply acknowledge
that and repent, He's waiting with open arms.*

LISA HARPER

PROTECT YOUR SOUL

*What do you benefit if you gain the whole
world but lose your own soul?*

MATTHEW 16:26

IN THIS VERSE, Jesus reminds us of what truly matters:
our eternal souls. We must protect our souls from worldly
desires that turn us away from following Jesus.

It doesn't matter how much success we attain, how
well our children do in school or sports, how much
money we make, or how big a home we own. All that
really matters in the end is our souls—because that's all
we can take with us when we leave this brief life on earth.

Gaining the whole world will gain us nothing. Let's
prepare for eternity by taking up our cross and faithfully
following our Savior.

*This morning my soul is greater than the
world since it possesses You, You whom
heaven and earth do not contain.*

MARGARET OF CORTONA

THE GREATEST COMMANDMENT

You must love the LORD your God with all your heart, all your soul, and all your mind.

MATTHEW 22:37

AN EXPERT IN RELIGIOUS LAW asked Jesus, "Teacher, which is the most important commandment?" (Matthew 22:36). Jesus responded that we are to love God with everything that we are. The more we love God, the more we will obey him and seek his guidance. In every decision we make, we can ask ourselves, "Am I doing this out of love for the Lord?"

In light of all God has done for us, our love for him should be wholehearted in response. And though we may fail at times, we can quickly repent and begin again—and live every second in love with our Savior.

> *Love Him totally who gave Himself totally for your love.*
>
> CLARE OF ASSISI

BE A GOOD STEWARD

The master was full of praise. "Well done,
my good and faithful servant."

MATTHEW 25:21

JESUS USED A PARABLE about three servants entrusted with money to teach about stewardship: the responsible use of resources. God gifts each of us with different resources—spiritual gifts, talents, abilities, money, and time—and he expects us to use them to support, grow, and bless his Kingdom.

You have been given certain resources. It is up to you to determine what they are and then decide what to do with them. When it's all said and done, don't you want to hear Jesus say, "Well done, my good and faithful servant"?

As male and female are made one in Jesus Christ,
so women receive an office in the Truth as well as
men, and they have a stewardship and must give an
account of their stewardship as well as the men.

ELIZABETH BATHURST

LOVE OTHERS, LOVE JESUS

I was hungry, and you fed me. I was thirsty,
and you gave me a drink. I was a stranger,
and you invited me into your home.

MATTHEW 25:35

MILLIONS OF PEOPLE in our world, many of them children, go to sleep hungry every night. Some of these
people live on the other side of the world. Some of them
live near you.

Jesus challenged us to do something about the needs
of others. When we feed someone, we are showing love
to Jesus. When we give someone a drink of water, we are
showing love to Jesus. When we show hospitality, we are
showing love to Jesus. How can you show love to Jesus
today?

I would rather die of hunger myself than
deny aid to the poor in this season, and thus
become guilty of their death before God.

QUEEN ELIZABETH OF PORTUGAL

NEVER FORSAKEN

*Jesus called out with a loud voice, "Eli, Eli,
lema sabachthani?" which means "My God,
my God, why have you abandoned me?"*

MATTHEW 27:46

AS HE HUNG DYING on the cross, Jesus experienced a
moment of complete loneliness and desolation. For just
an instant, God turned his face away from his dear Son.
And because he did, Jesus had to bear the pain of being
separated from his Father.

Jesus endured this pain in our place. Because of his
suffering, we do not have to experience the agony of being
separated from God. Jesus was forsaken on the cross so
that we will not be forsaken for eternity. Because of what
Jesus did for you on the cross, God will never abandon
you. God will never forget you. You are his child forever.

Thou hast never forsaken nor forgotten me.
KATHARINA VON BORA

A GREAT CALM

*When Jesus woke up, he rebuked the wind and
said to the waves, "Silence! Be still!" Suddenly
the wind stopped, and there was a great calm.*

MARK 4:39

TRY TO PICTURE IT: the boat bouncing around in the
waves. The panicked disciples waking Jesus up. Him
calming the storm with three words.

Jesus has complete power over nature. He also has
complete power over your heart. If you are dealing with a
storm right now, know that Jesus has the power to replace
that storm with peace. You don't need to panic. Just ask
him to take control of your circumstances. Then rest in
him as he calms the winds and waves in your life.

*His mighty voice commandeth
the raging waves within;
The floods of deepest anguish roll
backward at His will,
As o'er the storm ariseth His
mandate, "Peace, be still."*

CHARITIE L. BANCROFT

THE GIVER'S HEART

I tell you the truth, this poor widow has given more
than all the others who are making contributions.
For they gave a tiny part of their surplus, but she,
poor as she is, has given everything she had to live on.

MARK 12:43-44

WITH TODAY'S ubiquitous media, we often hear about generous donations to all kinds of charities and causes. Every day we're hearing about some wealthy philanthropist giving away millions of dollars. This can make us, and our pocketbooks, feel small. But we mustn't let these stories discourage us from giving whatever we can give to help those in need and to support our local church. Giving is an opportunity to worship, love, and honor God.

We learn from Jesus' teaching that it's not the size of the gift that matters—it is the condition of the giver's heart.

Nothing is small if God accepts it.
TERESA OF AVILA

BE ENCOURAGED

Be encouraged, my child! Your sins are forgiven.
MATTHEW 9:2

SOMETIMES WE CAN FEEL as though our courage tank is running low—as if we're running on courage fumes. Maybe the paralyzed man felt like this, lying on his bed unable to move, but people brought him to Jesus, who said, "Be encouraged! Your sins are forgiven."

We too can be encouraged by the clean slate that Jesus provides. Even on those really hard days, when we're exhausted, when we're overwhelmed by the to-do list— we have been forgiven! This fact can give us the courage to keep fighting, keep following Jesus, and keep claiming the joy that a relationship with him provides!

There is nothing at all that God won't forgive.
ANNE GRAHAM LOTZ

JESUS' BAPTISM

Jesus said, "It should be done, for we must carry out all that God requires." So John agreed to baptize him.

MATTHEW 3:15

WHEN JESUS ASKED John to baptize him, John the Baptist argued, "Why would I baptize you?" (see Matthew 3:14). No doubt he thought Jesus didn't need to be baptized, because he was the sinless Son of God. But Jesus insisted. By being baptized he showed that he would obey God in everything. We can be justified in Jesus because he lived a fully righteous life.

Baptism also represents Jesus' death and resurrection. When we are baptized, it's like we die and are resurrected with him. If you've been baptized, remember that moment right now, that huge step. Didn't it feel great to do what Jesus did so many years ago?

If you haven't been baptized, what are you waiting for?

In baptism we declare our loyalty to Christ the King and to His kingdom.

NANCY DEMOSS WOLGEMUTH

HOW TO ANSWER TEMPTATION

The Scriptures say, "People do not live by bread alone, but by every word that comes from the mouth of God."

MATTHEW 4:4

THE HOLY SPIRIT led Jesus into the wilderness, where Satan used trickery and deceit to tempt Jesus to sin. The devil twisted Scripture in order to use it for his own purposes.

But he was no match for Jesus, who knew the Word inside and out—because he is the Word of God. Jesus sets an inspiring example for us here by combating temptation with Scripture. We can do the same. But in order to do so, we have to know God's Word. Every word that comes from the mouth of God is useful to us.

> *Satan's strategy is effective because he sprinkles his poisonous brew with just enough veracity that we'll swallow it.*
>
> LISA HARPER

ONLY ONE GOD

*The Scriptures say, "You must
worship the LORD your God
and serve only him."*

MATTHEW 4:10

OF THE MANY temptations we face, idolatry can be the sneakiest. If we're not careful, we can idolize wealth, fitness, careers, hobbies, passions, and even relationships. But we can meet this type of temptation head-on with the Word of God.

The more time we spend with God in his Word, the less likely we are to be enticed by anything else. Nothing else can compare to our relationship with Jesus. Satan will try to convince us otherwise, but if we keep God and his Word in our hearts, we will stand strong.

*The only way that we can avoid the sin of idolatry
is by immersing ourselves in Spirit-enlightened
study of God through the Scripture.*

ELYSE M. FITZPATRICK

ASK AND BELIEVE

*I tell you, you can pray for anything, and if you
believe that you've received it, it will be yours.*

MARK 11:24

JESUS ENCOURAGES us to pray with unwavering faith.
When we consider what to ask for in prayer, we need to
remember God's loving character—he will never give us
anything that isn't ultimately good for us. While we don't
know God's plan in every circumstance, we can trust that
he will answer our prayers according to his perfect will.

God may not always answer your prayers in the ways
you imagine, but he does answer them. So when you
ask God to carry out his will in your life, believe he will
answer in the best way possible.

Go to the deeps of God's promise;
Ask freely of Him, and receive;
All good may be had for the asking,
If, seeking, you truly believe.

CARRIE E. BRECK

TO FISH FOR PEOPLE

Come, follow me, and I will show
you how to fish for people!

MATTHEW 4:19

JESUS SPOKE these words to fishermen. Imagine what they must have thought: *We're going to fish for people? What could that possibly mean? Let's go find out!*

Jesus obviously knew what he was doing, since they immediately dropped their nets and followed him. Would you have done the same? Would you today? If Jesus asks you to drop what you are doing in order to share his love with others, will you?

Magnificent Holy Father . . . Open our eyes to the vision You had in mind when You called us to be "fishers of men," and give us a heart to naturally draw others toward You. In Jesus' name. Amen.

SHANNON ETHRIDGE

FEBRUARY 6

THE BROKENHEARTED

*God blesses those who mourn,
for they will be comforted.*

MATTHEW 5:4

JESUS IS CLOSE to the brokenhearted. He has been there. He has felt unimaginable pain. And because he loves you so much, he is there with you in every tear, in every moment of anguish. You are never alone. And the day will come when you will never cry again.

We can put our love for Jesus into action when we see a sister who is crying. We can say, "I've been there." We can be with her in her tears and make sure she knows she is not alone. Do you know someone who is mourning, someone you could comfort today?

Our culture throws broken things away, but our Savior never does. He gently gathers all the pieces, and with His love and in His time, He puts us back together.

SHEILA WALSH

THE MERCIFUL

God blesses those who are merciful,
for they will be shown mercy.

MATTHEW 5:7

THERE IS NO WOMAN in the world who does not need God's mercy. Without it, we would have to pay the price for all our sins, for each and every time we have chosen our own way over God's way.

Thank God that he is merciful and does not require payment from us. In this verse Jesus is telling us that those who show mercy will be shown mercy. We can show mercy to others by forgiving them, even when they're not sorry. We can show mercy by trying to alleviate others' sufferings—visiting those who are sick or imprisoned. The best way to show mercy is to love others the way that our merciful God has loved us.

This is what God's mercy looks like toward you and me. . . . He has chosen not to give us what we deserve.

PRISCILLA SHIRER

THE PEACEMAKERS

God blesses those who work for peace,
for they will be called the children of God.

MATTHEW 5:9

WE CAN WORK for peace. Even when we are feeling small, powerless, and insignificant, we can work for peace. We can do it in the small moments and in the everyday, ordinary tasks of our lives. We can do it by choosing peace over conflict. We can do it by asking for forgiveness and forgiving others. We can do it by putting ourselves in others' shoes and putting their needs ahead of our own. We can work for peace with our friends, our neighbors, our fellow church members, and our families; in our communities, our country, and our world.

Next time you feel tempted to escalate a conflict, remember Jesus' words. *You* can be a peacemaker. You can start today.

Peace begins with a smile.
MOTHER TERESA

THE SALT OF THE EARTH

You are the salt of the earth.

MATTHEW 5:13

A SALT CRYSTAL is a small thing. But it can be mightily powerful. It can add flavor. It can preserve freshness. It can influence and change its surroundings. It is especially powerful when combined with other salt crystals.

Never feel that you are too small to have an influence on the world around you. You are not too small—because you believe in Christ. You are the salt of the earth. You add good flavor to every situation you are in. And you are a preserver of God's truth in a world full of lies. Work together with your brothers and sisters, and people will be drawn to God's goodness.

Home, church, community, and country desperately need the influence of women who know why they believe what they believe, grounded in the Word of God.

JEN WILKIN

THIS LITTLE LIGHT OF MINE

No one lights a lamp and then puts it under a basket. Instead, a lamp is placed on a stand, where it gives light to everyone in the house.

MATTHEW 5:15

USING THE METAPHOR of a lamp, Jesus tells us, "Don't be bashful!" If you are a follower of Jesus, God has cleansed you from sin and put his Holy Spirit within you. The beauty of your life lived righteously is like a bright light in a dark room.

So don't hide your light! Light up the world around you. Jesus gave you this light so you can shine it in the darkest corners of life. So go shine—and watch the darkness vanish.

The light in your soul is far greater than the darkness. Shine your light.

LAILAH GIFTY AKITA

SPREAD THE LIGHT

Let your good deeds shine out for all to see, so that everyone will praise your heavenly Father.

MATTHEW 5:16

WE SHOULDN'T DO good deeds in order to receive praise. We should do them so *God* will be praised. Our love for him and our desire to see him honored should motivate the kindness and goodness we extend to others.

When we do good deeds for others, often they will, in turn, do good deeds for others, who will do good deeds for others. God's love and light will fan out through humanity, spreading and multiplying exponentially. And that miraculous, spreading, growing, glowing light can start with you. Who can you bless today with your good deeds?

There are no doubt many who have illuminated our paths through this life. As we are obedient to his command there will be those whose lives we may brighten.

CHARLOTTE STEMPLE

AVOIDING SIN

You have heard the commandment that says,
"You must not commit adultery." But I say, anyone
who even looks at a woman with lust has already
committed adultery with her in her heart.

MATTHEW 5:27-28

THE RELIGIOUS LEADERS in Jesus' day acted like outward conformity to God's law was all that mattered. But Jesus said having lust in your heart was as bad as committing adultery.

Here's a little secret: sin usually starts out as an idea. If we let it take root, it will grow into something even worse. To avoid sinful actions, we need to avoid the sinful thoughts that pave the path for them. It's a lot easier to kick out a sinful thought than to deal with the consequences of acting on that sin. Do you want to walk with Jesus in peace? Don't let your mind go where it shouldn't!

Dealing with the sin in our hearts daily will protect
us from the bigger, longer-term, visible sins.

NANCY DEMOSS WOLGEMUTH

YOUR RIGHT HAND

When you give to someone in need, don't let your left hand know what your right hand is doing.

MATTHEW 6:3

WOMEN ARE OFTEN the unsung heroes. We organize, we plan, we cross the t's and dot the i's. We clean before, cook during, and pick up after. And if we're expecting a thank-you, well, it's usually unlikely we'll receive one.

But Jesus gently tells us not to be glory hounds, because our thank-you is coming. It's coming from God, when it will really matter. For now, our reward is knowing we can honor God by selflessly serving the people in our lives.

So, how can you sneakily bless someone today without anyone but Jesus knowing about it?

If I am happy to serve when no one is there to give me credit, I am truly working for the Lord.

JUNE GUNDEN

FEBRUARY 14

BEFORE YOU ASK

*Your Father knows exactly what you
need even before you ask him!*

MATTHEW 6:8

GOD KNOWS WHAT we need before we ask. What a comforting thought! He knows you're going to need a new computer before your old one dies. He knows you need a new job before you even realize it. He knows you need wisdom to make a critical decision before you even arrive at the crossroads.

And God knows the embarrassing stuff too: the stuff you need to apologize for, the temptation you're currently facing, the junk you need to be set free from.

Do you ever hesitate to go to him with your requests? Remember this: you're not going to shock him with anything, and he wants to hear from you. He created you, after all.

*God knows you better than you know yourself
and has reached his verdict: he loves you still.*

DEBBIE ALSDORF

THY WILL BE DONE

*May your Kingdom come soon. May your will
be done on earth, as it is in heaven.*

MATTHEW 6:10

WHEN JESUS TAUGHT his followers how they should pray,
he put praying for God's Kingdom and God's will toward
the beginning of the list, ahead of praying for personal
needs. Sometimes our prayers resemble grocery lists of
things we want. This isn't necessarily wrong; we should
tell God our desires. But we must ask for these things
according to God's will, putting God's Kingdom first.
This shows that God himself is our first love, not what
he can give us.

Trust him to give you what you really need, not what
you think you need. Don't you want God to bless you
according to his wildest dreams, rather than yours?

*To be formed into Christ is to fully desire—and
fully commit—to the coming of God's kingdom.*

JEN POLLOCK MICHEL

NOT A SINGLE MOMENT

Can all your worries add a single
moment to your life?

MATTHEW 6:27

WOMEN CAN BE such talented worriers. We worry
because we love so much. We love our families. We love
our friends. We want what's best for them.

But worrying won't help anyone. We can worry ourselves silly, and it won't change a thing. It won't keep
anyone safe, and it won't put money in the bank. It won't
heal anyone, and it won't make things turn out the way
we want.

Jesus tells us *not* to worry. He tells us to just let him
be in charge, because he knows what he's doing far better
than we do. Instead of worrying, why don't we focus our
energy on praying? That will help our family and friends
far more than our anxiety ever could.

The answer to deep anxiety is the
deep adoration of God.

ANN VOSKAMP

SEEK HIM FIRST

*Seek the Kingdom of God above all else, and live
righteously, and he will give you everything you need.*

MATTHEW 6:33

ISN'T IT GREAT when Jesus makes it simple? The first thing
we're supposed to do is seek God, seek his Kingdom. We
are to live righteously, which we can't do on our own. So
we need to live our lives walking in Christ's righteousness,
which he's given to us.

And then God will give us everything we need. We
don't have to worry about any of it. We don't have to
try to put the pieces together. We just have to seek God,
who made the puzzle, and walk with Jesus. Simple, right?
Thank you, Jesus!

*When praying
for what is best for Me and My kingdom
in all things pertaining to you,
you'll always have what is best for you.*

MARIE CHAPIAN

UNEXPLAINABLE

The wind blows wherever it wants. Just as you can hear the wind but can't tell where it comes from or where it is going, so you can't explain how people are born of the Spirit.

JOHN 3:8

WE CAN'T SEE THE WIND, but we can see the effects it has on the world around us. That's what the working of the Holy Spirit is like in our lives.

Sometimes the Holy Spirit's working is like the majestic strength of a hurricane. But more often, the Holy Spirit presents himself as that slight breeze that refreshes you on a hot day. He is a whisper only you can hear in a noisy world, and when you listen to that voice, you can't help but transform.

He came in tongues of living flame,
To teach, convince, subdue;
All powerful as the wind he came,
As viewless too.

HARRIET AUBER

KNOWN BY OUR FRUIT

*Just as you can identify a tree by its fruit, so
you can identify people by their actions.*

MATTHEW 7:20

PEOPLE ARE OBSERVING the way we live our lives. If they
see that we love our families, we love strangers, and we
serve in our communities, they will recognize that we
belong to Christ.

This does not mean we need to be perfect. It does
mean that we should strive to walk closely with Jesus,
so that his love shines from us. A woman who lives in
love with Jesus will undoubtedly have tangible, visible
evidence of that love in her life. Put Christ first in everything, and beautiful, sweet, delicious fruit will grow.

*Our authenticity (or lack thereof) is made
evident by the fruit that our lives are bearing.*

CHRISTINE CAINE

DO THE WILL OF GOD

Not everyone who calls out to me, "Lord! Lord!"
will enter the Kingdom of Heaven. Only those who
actually do the will of my Father in heaven will enter.

MATTHEW 7:21

JESUS DOES NOT want lip service. If we say we belong to him, then we need to live according to God's will. This means relying on the Holy Spirit to help us obey and repenting immediately and sincerely when we disobey. It means loving God with all that we are and loving others more than we love ourselves.

This is how we demonstrate that our faith is alive and well. This is how we enter God's presence.

To love God is to love His will. It is to wait quietly
for life to be measured by One who knows us
through and through. It is to be content with
His timing and His wise appointment.

ELISABETH ELLIOT

THE ACT OF BELIEVING

*Jesus said to the Roman officer, "Go back home.
Because you believed, it has happened." And the
young servant was healed that same hour.*

MATTHEW 8:13

WHEN A ROMAN OFFICER asked Jesus to heal his servant,
Jesus said, "I'll come right now." But the officer said,
"You don't need to come. You have the power to heal
from right where you are" (see Matthew 8:7-8). This
impressed Jesus. This man had enough faith in Jesus to
not limit Jesus' power. Jesus acknowledged the man's faith
and healed his servant.

Sometimes we limit Jesus' power with our own lack
of faith. We have certain expectations, and we don't ask
or hope beyond them. What could happen in our lives if
we believed that Jesus could truly do *anything*?

*Nothing on earth compares to the
strength God is willing to interject into
lives caught in the act of believing.*

BETH MOORE

SIT WITH ME

*Those who are victorious will sit with me
on my throne, just as I was victorious and
sat with my Father on his throne.*

REVELATION 3:21

ONE OF THE LOFTIEST promises in the entire Bible is that not only will Jesus allow his saints a seat on his throne, but they will actually get to sit *with* him.

When you consider that Jesus paid for all our sins, this promise seems even more incredible. Jesus is going to share his throne with people so unworthy that he had to redeem them from death. Yet those who have overcome temptation, who have finished the race, who have served Jesus in this life will be sitting with him in the next life.

*My Master, my Master, my joy is in Thee,
In Thee is my help, Lord, and only in Thee.*

MARGARET E. SANGSTER

BUT FIRST

*Don't imagine that I came to bring peace to the
earth! I came not to bring peace, but a sword.*

MATTHEW 10:34

JESUS IS THE Prince of Peace. If he is your Lord and
Savior, then he is reigning in peace in your heart right
now, and eventually he will reign from his eternal throne
in perfect peace. *But first*, there will be conflict—because
the gospel brings it. There will be those who don't want
to hear the gospel, or don't want to accept it, or don't
want to be accountable to it. These people might be your
friends or relatives.

Don't lose heart. Jesus told you this would happen,
and this conflict is only temporary. Jesus' brothers and
sisters will spend eternity with him, and a peaceful forever it will be.

*The gospel will bring reactions and
responses—even from within our families.
Disciples must be ready for them.*

JILL BRISCOE

I WILL GIVE YOU REST

*Come to me, all of you who are weary and carry
heavy burdens, and I will give you rest.*

MATTHEW 11:28

CARING FOR OUR FAMILIES, serving in our churches, and
working in our communities are good works, but if we're
doing them in order to earn Jesus' love, we're doing it
backward. Good works don't lead to grace: grace leads
to good works.

Jesus wants you to *rest in him.* Come to him. Give
him your cares, your worries, and your problems. He'll
take care of it all! Then you will be free to do those good
works. And when you start serving from a rested, peaceful place, you will be so much better equipped to love
others and bring glory to God!

*Real rest comes with knowing the grace of our
salvation in Jesus. We don't have to earn it.*

SHEILA WALSH

JESUS' YOKE

Take my yoke upon you. Let me teach you,
because I am humble and gentle at heart, and
you will find rest for your souls. For my yoke is
easy to bear, and the burden I give you is light.

MATTHEW 11:29-30

FARMERS YOKE OXEN so they can pull a heavy load. But Jesus says the burden he gives us is light. Compared to the heavy weight of sin we used to carry, Jesus' one requirement is simple: believe in him and let him teach you.

When two oxen are yoked together, one cannot veer off in its own direction on a whim. If you are yoked to Jesus, you're going in his direction. You're going to do things his way. Only by wearing Jesus' yoke will you find rest for your soul in this busy, crazy, scary world.

The yoke spoken of in this passage is fashioned
of discipline and discipleship; its lining is love.

DIANE HEAD

A TEENY SEED

The Kingdom of Heaven is like a mustard seed planted in a field. It is the smallest of all seeds, but it becomes the largest of garden plants; it grows into a tree, and birds come and make nests in its branches.

MATTHEW 13:31-32

A TEENY SEED can quickly grow into a plant that can take over an entire garden. The Kingdom of God is meant to grow, and the more it grows, the more it has potential to grow—exponentially reaching new believers and crossing new borders.

Never underestimate what you can accomplish for the Kingdom of God when you share your faith with someone. You may feel small, but God can do big things through you.

I never lose an opportunity of urging a practical beginning, however small, for it is wonderful how often in such matters the mustard-seed germinates and roots itself.

FLORENCE NIGHTINGALE

YES, COME

Yes, come.

MATTHEW 14:29

THE DISCIPLES SAW Jesus walking toward them on the surface of the sea, and Peter said, "Prove it's you by telling me to come to you!" (see Matthew 14:26-28).

And Jesus said, "Come."

Would you have been surprised if you'd been in Peter's shoes? Are you surprised now when Jesus invites you to do something that seems impossible?

Peter walked on the water. Jesus would not have said "Come" if he wasn't going to enable him to do so. And he won't say "Come" to you unless he's going to empower you to do what he commands. So next time you're asked to accomplish the impossible, don't think, *I can't do that.* Know that you *can*—or Jesus never would have issued the invitation.

You make my footsteps and my path secure.
So walking on water is just the beginning.

AMANDA COOK

FOCUS

You have so little faith. . . . Why did you doubt me?

MATTHEW 14:31

PETER WAS DOING just fine. He was actually walking on the water toward Jesus. And he would have kept on going *if* he hadn't shifted his attention from Jesus to the wind and waves, *if* he hadn't looked away from his Savior to focus on his circumstances (see Matthew 14:29-30).

Don't we do the same thing? We live and walk in Jesus' miracle-working power, but then we cast a quick glance at the situation around us and freak out. What would happen if we never took our eyes off Jesus? What miracles would he have us participate in?

Turn your eyes upon Jesus,
Look full in His wonderful face,
And the things of earth will grow strangely dim,
In the light of His glory and grace.

HELEN H. LEMMEL

SOMETHING GLORIOUS

If you try to hang on to your life, you will lose it. But if you give up your life for my sake, you will save it.

MATTHEW 16:25

WHEN YOU CHOOSE to follow Jesus, you save your life—not just your *eternal* life but also your *right now* life. When you decide to prioritize loving God and loving others, everything changes. Life becomes richer, simpler, and more authentic. It becomes full of joy and laughter and peace.

Life is still hard. Bad things still happen. We will still struggle. But when we are in the midst of the pain, we can choose to give up our lives for Jesus, and that decision turns our pain into something glorious.

When we become absorbed in something demanding and worthwhile above and beyond ourselves, happiness seems to be there as a by-product of the self-giving.

CATHERINE MARSHALL

THE TRANSFIGURATION

Get up. . . . Don't be afraid.
MATTHEW 17:7

WOULD YOU HAVE fallen down in fear in the presence of Jesus' glory? Peter, James, and John saw Jesus transform right before their eyes. Imagine! His face shone as bright as the sun, and his clothes became a brilliant white. Then Moses and Elijah appeared and started talking to Jesus (see Matthew 17:1-6).

As if that weren't enough, God then spoke to them out of a cloud: "Listen to Jesus." No wonder they were terrified! But Jesus, ever compassionate, gently touched them and told them to get up, almost as if to say, "You're okay. You're with me."

Our relationship with the radiant, glorious Son of God allows us to unashamedly and boldly stand in the Father's presence.

The same Savior who gave three disciples a foretaste of his kingdom wants to make our life radiate with his glory as he transforms us into his image.
DIANNE NEAL MATTHEWS

LIKE LITTLE CHILDREN

*I tell you the truth, unless you turn from your
sins and become like little children, you will
never get into the Kingdom of Heaven.*

MATTHEW 18:3

YOUNG CHILDREN fully rely on their parents or caretakers
to provide for their needs. This dependence is the type of
faith Jesus wants from us. The world seeks to trample this
kind of faith. We are taught to value independence and
self-reliance. If we depend on ourselves for salvation—or
for anything—then we lack faith in the one who provides
all we need.

It's not too late for us, no matter how old we are, to
develop a childlike faith. Place your full trust in Jesus
today. Count on him to care for you.

*Then let me know the freshening
found in simple, childlike prayer,
when the kneeling soul knows surely
that a listening Lord is there.*

RUTH BELL GRAHAM

THE LOST SHEEP

*If a man has a hundred sheep and one of them
wanders away, what will he do? Won't he
leave the ninety-nine others on the hills and
go out to search for the one that is lost?*

MATTHEW 18:12

SOMETIMES WOMEN feel they've strayed too far away
from God and will never find their way back. You're never
too far gone. No matter how far off the path you get, the
Shepherd will still search for you. No matter how many
wrong turns you've taken or how long you've been wandering, Jesus can still save you. And he wants to.

He also wants to save the women who cross your path
today—*all* of them. Sometimes we encounter someone
who seems beyond help. But she's not. Jesus loves her,
too. And she can experience his love through you.

*I suppose sometimes it takes getting lost
to enjoy the joy of being found.*
TRICIA GOYER

HOW TO HANDLE THE HURT

*If another believer sins against you, go privately
and point out the offense. If the other person listens
and confesses it, you have won that person back.*

MATTHEW 18:15

IF YOU SPEND any amount of time with other people,
someone will hurt you. And you will hurt others. It is
inevitable, because all people are broken sinners in need
of a Savior. But Jesus plainly tells us how to handle these
situations (see also Matthew 18:16-17). Notice that he
doesn't say, "Get all puffed up with self-righteousness
and start a big fight that will effectively halt all Kingdom
work."

Rather than hold a grudge against another believer,
let's seek reconciliation and restoration of the relationship.

*No matter how negative the circumstance, we
can never go wrong by taking the high road.*

GINA DUKE

JOINED

Since they are no longer two but one, let no one
split apart what God has joined together.

MATTHEW 19:6

MARRIAGE MATTERS to Jesus: he spoke about it multiple times. He says that in marriage, two individuals become one. But achieving that oneness in marriage is hard, because it involves humans, a man and a woman, trying to love each other selflessly and sacrificially like Jesus taught. Loving this way is a mighty high calling. So when you're struggling, call out to Jesus. Lean on him. Make him the center of everything, even your marriage.

If you are single, divorced, or widowed, know that Jesus is with you there. If you are married, know that Jesus is with you in your marriage.

Then while we live, in love let's so persevere
That when we live no more, we may live ever.

ANNE BRADSTREET

A HUNDRED TIMES

Everyone who has given up houses or brothers or sisters or father or mother or children or property, for my sake, will receive a hundred times as much in return and will inherit eternal life.

MATTHEW 19:29

NO ONE WANTS to think about giving up their homes or hometowns, their possessions, or especially their loved ones. Sometimes Jesus asks us to let go of these things for his sake. But there is good news! When we give up something for Jesus, our reward will be great—not only material things but also an eternity with Jesus.

Nothing on this earth, nothing we could give up, can compare to the reward Jesus has in store for those who love and serve him.

Whatever sacrifice we make for Jesus will be worth it. We have his promise that we will be repaid a hundredfold—and that's a wise investment.

DIANNE NEAL MATTHEWS

ANGER

*The Scriptures declare, "My Temple will
be called a house of prayer," but you have
turned it into a den of thieves!*

MATTHEW 21:13

JESUS STORMED into the Temple and began to drive out
the money changers, who were taking advantage of other
people and using the Temple for their own gain. Jesus'
actions show that it is acceptable to feel anger at evil.
Even Jesus got angry when the situation warranted it.

In this life, we will see bad things happen, and it's
not a sin to feel anger toward those things. Rather than
bottle anger up inside until it grows into something we
can't control, we can use our anger, as Jesus did, to effect
change for the better.

*Anger isn't a bad emotion. In fact, it
can often cause people to make positive
changes in the world around them.*

GERALYN PETERSON

A GIFT THAT WON'T BE FORGOTTEN

*She has poured this perfume on me
to prepare my body for burial.*

MATTHEW 26:12

A WOMAN CAME to Jesus and poured a jar of expensive perfume on his head. Imagine her courage! The onlookers criticized her actions because they didn't understand the meaning behind her act of worship (see Matthew 26:7-9). If only they had known that Jesus was about to die. He was about to be sacrificed *for them*.

Sometimes, when we truly seek God, he will ask us to do things that onlookers don't understand. Sometimes even *we* don't understand why God wants us to do something. But if our actions are done in love, then Jesus accepts them as a gift of worship.

*It's comforting to know that our gifts are
acceptable, accepted and appreciated
by the Lord when given in love.*

SUE RICHARDS

DO IT

*Even more blessed are all who hear the
word of God and put it into practice.*

LUKE 11:28

IT'S AN EASY TRAP to fall into, especially for those of us
who have been following Jesus for a while. We hear the
sermons on Sundays, we sing the songs, we even teach the
Sunday school lessons, but how much of it are we actually
obeying? Have we become numb to the Word of God?

We can never know it all. There's always something
new to learn. And there's always some new way to put
God's Word into action. Jesus doesn't want us to just *hear*
the Word. He wants us to *do* it!

*I need to listen well to what God is saying.
I look for one verse that I can savor word by
word, letting it sink in deeply . . . interrupting
me, rearranging me, redirecting me.*

LYSA TERKEURST

ALWAYS

Be sure of this: I am with you always,
even to the end of the age.

MATTHEW 28:20

SOMETIMES WE CAN'T *FEEL* Jesus' presence, power, influence, justice, or love. It is at these times that we need to trust him to keep his word. He promised he would be with us always—during good times and bad—and he does not break his promises. So even though we see horrific things happening in our world, even though we see loved ones suffering and injustice running rampant, he is still here. He is still working. We just need to trust in his wisdom and his timing.

God doesn't always protect those He loves
from suffering . . . but He does promise in
His Word that He will be present with us in
the midst of our suffering and pain.

ANNE GRAHAM LOTZ

FORGIVEN

My child, your sins are forgiven.

MARK 2:5

A PARALYZED MAN'S friends cut a hole in the roof so he could get to Jesus and receive his mercy (see Mark 2:3-4). It's a vivid portrait of how each of us comes to Jesus: desperately, by any means necessary. And when the paralyzed man finally saw Jesus, Jesus didn't ask him to jump through any hoops. There were no classes to take, no lengthy applications to fill out. Jesus simply looked at the man, saw his heart, and said, "You are forgiven."

It's a done deal. There is no "if." There is only forgiveness. That day, that man's life changed. His eternity changed. The day we come before Jesus, desperate for his mercy, our lives change too—forever.

I could hardly comprehend His offer:
I'd bring what I had, He'd bring the rest.

GLORIA GAITHER

BE REAL

Healthy people don't need a doctor—sick people do. I have come to call not those who think they are righteous, but those who know they are sinners.

MARK 2:17

WHO DO WE THINK we are fooling? If we were perfect, we wouldn't need Jesus, so why do we pretend we've got it all together? No woman is drawn to someone who acts holier-than-thou: women are drawn to real women— those who openly admit they have flaws and faults, who don't deny the fact that life is messy sometimes, and who are unashamed of their need of a Savior.

Want to draw others toward the love of Jesus? Be real. You never know whom your scars may bless.

Live your life transparently so other women will see that Jesus loves the weak, the weary, the wounded, and the sinner, and perhaps they, too, will be emboldened to stop faking it.

ELYSE M. FITZPATRICK

LORD OVER EVERYTHING

The Son of Man is Lord, even over the Sabbath!

MARK 2:28

THE PHARISEES ACCUSED Jesus' disciples of sinning, simply because they were picking some grain on the Sabbath (see Mark 2:23-24). Such nitpickers! Obviously, they had no idea who they were talking to. Jesus *created* the laws they were trying to manipulate, and he had come to accomplish their purpose (see Matthew 5:17).

In his response, Jesus denounces legalism. There is no law, no rule, no program, no tradition that is more powerful than the Son of God. And if we start to put such human institutions above God, we quickly go astray, just like the Pharisees.

Must we always comment on life? Can it not simply be lived in the reality of Christ's terms of contact with the Father, with joy and peace, fear and love full to the fingertips in their turn, without incessant drawing of lessons and making of rules?

ELISABETH ELLIOT

ANYONE WHO DOES GOD'S WILL

*Anyone who does God's will is my
brother and sister and mother.*

MARK 3:35

WHAT AN HONOR to be called a sister of Jesus! And all we have to do first is do God's will. This may seem like a tall order, but Jesus wouldn't have said it unless it were possible.

We can follow God's will by seeking his heart and his desires, in his Word, through prayer, and through the wisdom of other brothers and sisters in Christ. Even if we step out of his will, if we are seeking him, we will know we've gotten off track, and the Holy Spirit will help us get right back on.

When we walk in God's will, our lives are so much richer. We are free and full of peace and joy as sisters of Jesus.

*Fullness of joy is discovered only
in the emptying of will.*

ANN VOSKAMP

FERTILE SOIL

Other seeds fell on fertile soil, and they sprouted,
grew, and produced a crop that was thirty, sixty, and
even a hundred times as much as had been planted!

MARK 4:8

IF YOU HAVE PUT your faith in Jesus, then this verse describes you! Not everyone chooses to follow Jesus, and those people are like the others described in this parable, the ones whose faith died away quickly because of rocks or thorns (see Mark 4:3-7).

But not you. *You* are the *fertile soil.* You are the one who is going to grow in leaps and bounds, who is going to produce fruit and multiply Jesus' Kingdom. *You* are the one who is going to do things beyond what you could have dreamed when that seed first fell on you.

If you commit yourself to living according
to His Word your potential will be unlocked,
and in time, what may look small now
will grow into something significant.

CHRISTINE CAINE

THE SECRETS OF THE KINGDOM

*You are permitted to understand the secret
of the Kingdom of God. But I use parables
for everything I say to outsiders.*

MARK 4:11

JESUS WAS GIVING his disciples the inside scoop. They were ready for it, but not everyone is. That's because we each must start with belief. We must choose to put our faith in Jesus before he will begin to lift the veil. But once we choose him, he shows us a new way of living, of thinking, of loving—a new way of *being*.

So when people don't understand the things you believe, encourage them to start at the beginning, where you started. Introduce them to Jesus.

*It's a delight for Me to tell you of the wonders
in store for you
when you live vitally united to Me,
and when My words
live in your thoughts as
permanent fixtures.*

MARIE CHAPIAN

CLOSE ATTENTION

*Pay close attention to what you hear. The closer
you listen, the more understanding you will
be given—and you will receive even more.*

MARK 4:24

JESUS TOLD HIS FOLLOWERS, "Pay close attention and *listen. Then* you will understand." But so often we want the easy solution. So often we're looking for quick answers in the Bible index while juggling sippy cups and car pools. This isn't seeking the way Jesus describes it.

Jesus is telling us to *pay* attention, to give of ourselves—our whole minds—to the teaching at hand. We can read the Bible and meditate on what we've just read. We can pray and listen for the response. We can really focus on biblical teaching. In doing these things, in really *listening*, we will be gifted with understanding.

*When the Word is read, that's God talking. [We should
listen] with a sense of awe and wonder that God is
here in this place and God is actually speaking to me.*

NANCY DEMOSS WOLGEMUTH

UNFATHOMABLE

*I have loved you even as the Father has
loved me. Remain in my love.*

JOHN 15:9

WE CAN'T FATHOM how much God loves his Son. We
just know it is an infinite, unstoppable, supernatural love.
This is the same love that Jesus lavishes on us. And he not
only offers us this love but also instructs us to remain in
it—to live in the knowledge of it day by day.

We never have to exist a single second apart from the
unfathomable, indescribable love of our Savior.

*Put together all the tenderest love you know of . . .
and heap upon it all the love of all the loving
human hearts in the world, and then multiply
it by infinity, and you will begin perhaps to
have some faint glimpses of what the love of
God in Christ Jesus is. And this is grace.*

HANNAH WHITALL SMITH

IF I COULD JUST
TOUCH HIS ROBE

Daughter, your faith has made you well.
Go in peace. Your suffering is over.

MARK 5:34

THE WOMAN HAD BEEN bleeding for twelve years. She was financially devastated and a social outcast. Yet she knew that Jesus had the power to change her life. So she fought her way through the crowd and touched his robe. And immediately she was healed (see Mark 5:25-29).

Many of us can identify with her desperation. What Jesus said to her, he will say to us. He will know our faith, heal us, and fill us with his peace that exceeds our understanding. Miracles do happen. All you have to do is reach for his robe and fall to your knees at his feet.

When we put feet to our faith, believing we'll
find an answer, that's when miracles happen.

LIZ CURTIS HIGGS

So Simple, yet So True

Don't be afraid. Just have faith.

MARK 5:36

Jairus had just been told that his twelve-year-old daughter was dead (see Mark 5:35). And Jesus told him, "Don't be afraid. Just have faith." Can you imagine? If those words hadn't come from Jesus, they would sound pretty irritating! Jairus didn't know that Jesus had power over death. But Jairus soon learned that those seemingly simplistic words had great power in his current circumstances to bring peace.

We can find peace too. Whatever horrible threat, awful news, or fearsome diagnoses we face, we can apply these words: "Don't be afraid. Just have faith." And we, too, will find the peace of Jesus.

Things which sound like platitudes become vital, living and powerful when you have to learn them in dark tunnels.

ELISABETH ELLIOT

HOMETOWN PROPHETS

*A prophet is honored everywhere except
in his own hometown and among his
relatives and his own family.*

MARK 6:4

THE BAD NEWS: you might be dishonored by those closest to you. Your family and neighbors may ignore God's
working in you and try to disparage your faith. The good
news: it happened to Jesus, too. You're in good company.

The more you live for Jesus, the more you will be
aware of this truth. The more you grow in him, the more
people may try to deny your growth. It's all right. What
they say doesn't matter. What matters is what Jesus says.
And he says you're his sister, he chose you, he loves you,
and he will enable you to do great things for him.

*Jesus' identity, worth and power came
from His Heavenly Father and not from
the validation of any earthly being.*

RACHEL OLSEN

JUST YOU AND JESUS

*Let's go off by ourselves to a quiet
place and rest awhile.*

MARK 6:31

WHEN JESUS SUGGESTED taking time to rest, the exhausted disciples must have looked to the heavens and exclaimed, "Thank you, God!" Can you imagine trying to keep up with Jesus? But Jesus tells his followers that we are not supposed to work ourselves to death. God designed us to *need* rest. If we don't unplug from the busyness and spend time just resting with Jesus, we will burn out and be useless to him, not to mention miserable.

Sometimes we need to literally schedule rest time in. We need to physically write it on the calendar—quiet time in the Word; time in prayer; a walk in the woods; coffee with a sister—and then *keep* that appointment.

*Strength of my heart, I rest in Thee,
Fulfil Thy purposes through me.*
AMY CARMICHAEL

WHO DO YOU SAY I AM?

[Jesus] asked them, "But who do you say I am?"
Peter replied, "You are the Messiah."

MARK 8:29

JESUS ASKED HIS DISCIPLES to consider the most important question of all, the one each of us will have to answer for herself. *Who is Jesus?* If we say that he is the risen Messiah, the Son of God, then we are well on our way to eternal life. If we say anything else, we're not quite there yet.

It is fashionable these days to call Jesus other things: a prophet, a great teacher, a political activist. Those of us who know the truth need to hold fast to our faith. And we need to pray for those who have not yet believed the truth about our Savior.

Our relationship with God and the eternal destiny
of our souls depend on what we believe about Jesus's
identity. We can't afford to get the answer wrong.

DIANNE NEAL MATTHEWS

YOU FAITHLESS PEOPLE!

You faithless people! How long must I be with you?

MARK 9:19

THE DISCIPLES HAD failed to free a boy from a demon (see Mark 9:17-18). But Jesus doesn't call them "failures"; he calls them "faithless." If they had had faith, they wouldn't have failed. Jesus asks, "How long must I be with you?" In other words, "I've shown you how to do this! How many more times do I have to show you? All you have to do is believe!"

What are we failing to accomplish because we don't believe? Are we limiting Jesus' power in our lives with our faithlessness?

Beloved, we needn't wonder why there is so much evil and suffering in the world when people who claim to know God have stopped believing in His power.

LIZ CURTIS HIGGS

ASK ANYWAY

*What do you mean, "If I can"? Anything
is possible if a person believes.*

MARK 9:23

A DESPERATE FATHER brought his demon-possessed son
before Jesus and said, "If you can, please heal him" (see
Mark 9:17-22). Jesus said, "If I can?" Of course Jesus
could heal the boy! Jesus knew it, but this father didn't
know it yet. Still, Jesus freed the man's son from the spirit
that bound him.

Even when we can't completely believe that Jesus can
do something, we can still come before him and ask. This
father wasn't quite confident, but he asked Jesus anyway.
We can come to Jesus and say, "I don't quite understand
how you can possibly heal this marriage, cure this cancer,
or pull this lost heart to you, but I'm asking you to do
it anyway."

*God . . . is capable of tremendously more than we have
witnessed. I have become utterly convinced that we see
so little primarily because we believe Him for so little.*

BETH MOORE

LOVE IS THE PROOF

*Your love for one another will prove to
the world that you are my disciples.*

JOHN 13:35

JESUS DIDN'T SAY, "They will know you by your picket signs, your articulate arguments, or your generalized judgments." He said, "They will know you are mine by the way you *love* one another."

But if we run around trying to love everybody else, we'll burn out before we accomplish much. This isn't what Jesus intended. We need to be walking in Jesus' love every single day. We need to be living in his love and letting him love us. When we do that, his love will naturally spill out into those around us. And *that's* what people will recognize as authentic. They'll say, "What's up with those people? They're all so *loving*!"

*A life contemplating the blessings of Christ
becomes a life acting the love of Christ.*

ANN VOSKAMP

A SIMPLE QUESTION

What do you want me to do for you?

MARK 10:51

JESUS HAD TRAVELED many miles, and a large crowd trailed after him. Amid all the mayhem, a beggar hollered his name (see Mark 10:46-50). Jesus asked, "What do you want me to do for you?" It's a scary question for most of us to ask, because there's a good chance someone will want us to do something. Yet this is what Jesus did.

When a sister is overwhelmed by circumstances, emotions, or stress, it's a great question to ask her. She might answer, "Nothing," or she might tell you exactly how you can meet her need.

> *In a day when servanthood is dying for lack of examples and we get all tied up in theological knots over even the meaning of the word, we might do well to start where Jesus did—with a simple question, "What can I do for you?"*

RUTH SENTER

FIRST, FORGIVE

*When you are praying, first forgive anyone
you are holding a grudge against, so that your
Father in heaven will forgive your sins, too.*

MARK 11:25

THERE ARE MANY REASONS why forgiving others is good
for us. One of these reasons is that *not* forgiving is incredibly unhealthy. And what does refusing to forgive really
accomplish? Does it prove to someone that we are right?
But who is really watching? Does anyone even care?

Why would we want to pour so much of ourselves
into something that will reap nothing but heartache,
especially when we could be using our energy for much
better things? Jesus teaches us to forgive so that we can
be set free from our own sins. Forgiveness frees us to live
our lives in peace and to joyfully serve Christ and other
people.

The beginning of forgiveness is often exhaustion.
ANNE LAMOTT

ANYONE WHO BELIEVES

Go into all the world and preach the Good News to everyone. Anyone who believes and is baptized will be saved. But anyone who refuses to believe will be condemned.

MARK 16:15-16

JESUS WANTS US to believe and to be baptized. And it's truly as simple as just believing in him! When you believe in Jesus, you will want to be baptized to let everyone know about your faith.

You can't believe in someone you've never heard about. We can make sure that the people we know the best and see the most often have that chance to *believe in* Jesus—because we know there is nothing better than growing in a relationship with Jesus and knowing we are saved.

At the end of our life, what will matter most is whether we had a personal relationship with Christ.

DIANNE NEAL MATTHEWS

UNCONDITIONAL

If you love only those who love you, why
should you get credit for that? Even
sinners love those who love them!

LUKE 6:32

JESUS CHALLENGED his followers to a new kind of love. Of course we love our children, our spouses, our friends. But what does that prove? The love of Jesus is an unconditional love. He challenges us to love people who will *not* love us back.

Yes, this kind of love opens us up to potential mistreatment. This kind of love got Jesus crucified. But this is the kind of love that represents God, who is love. This is the kind of love that people will notice and desire to learn more about.

Wouldn't it be unfortunate if we made it to the end
of our lives and only loved those who loved us? What
might we miss in those harder places of our faith?

SUZIE ELLER

LOVE AS GOD HAS LOVED YOU

*You must be compassionate, just as
your Father is compassionate.*

LUKE 6:36

NOTICE JESUS DIDN'T SAY, "You *should* be compassionate" or "Be compassionate once in a while." He used the word *must*. It's a command. But compassion doesn't come easily for many of us. Sometimes we look at a person and see only her mistakes or flaws.

But this is not how God sees her. Jesus said that we should care about others the way that God cares about them. This means trying to see them through God's eyes. You can always say, "God, please let me see her the way you see her." And when God gives you a glimpse of that version of her, a glimpse of his precious child, you can't help but feel compassion.

*We should be the first ones to walk alongside
those who are suffering, with hope and
gentleness, compassion and love.*

SARAH BESSEY

TEARS ON HIS FEET

*I tell you, her sins—and they are many—have been
forgiven, so she has shown me much love. But a
person who is forgiven little shows only little love.*

LUKE 7:47

ONE DAY A WOMAN came to Jesus. Luke calls her an
"immoral woman." As she knelt in front of Jesus, her
grateful tears fell on his feet. She wiped her tears away
with her hair and put perfume on Jesus' feet (see
Luke 7:37-38).

Many women can relate to her adoration. A person
who has been forgiven for a lot shows a *lot* of love. Those
of us who are aware of how much our sins helped pound
the nails into Jesus' body know the sweet relief of being
set free.

*If we reflect on how much our forgiveness cost God
and how little we deserve it, we'll think that no
expression of love is too lavish for such a Savior.*

DIANNE NEAL MATTHEWS

YOU LEAD; I'LL FOLLOW

*If any of you wants to be my follower,
you must give up your own way, take up
your cross daily, and follow me.*

LUKE 9:23

WE CANNOT REMAIN the captain of our lives and follow Jesus at the same time. We cannot be charting our own course while following his. Instead, we must surrender our ways, will, and wants to him.

And this has to be done daily, because our stubborn old selves keep popping up and trying to interfere. Then we have to take a deep breath and say, "Jesus, your will is the way. You lead, I'll follow. Even if it means the death of my body, I will follow you into eternity."

We can willingly be crucified with Christ because we are raised to walk in resurrection life. Biblical self-denial will never fail to be for us rather than against us, whether here or in eternity.

BETH MOORE

THE GOOD SAMARITAN

"Which of these three would you say
was a neighbor to the man who was
attacked by bandits?" Jesus asked.
The man replied, "The one who showed him mercy."
Then Jesus said, "Yes, now go and do the same."

LUKE 10:36-37

THE PARABLE OF the Good Samaritan suggests that we should be ready to show mercy to our neighbors and that those neighbors could be anyone we meet, anywhere, at any time.

How can we show mercy? How can we alleviate someone's suffering? How can we help someone in need? Which neighbor can you show mercy to today?

If I could give you information of my life, it would be
to show you how a woman of very ordinary ability
has been led by God, in strange and unaccustomed
paths, to do in his service what he has done in her.

FLORENCE NIGHTINGALE

SITTING AT THE FEET OF CHRIST

You are worried and upset over all these details!
There is only one thing worth being concerned about.

LUKE 10:41-42

WHILE MARY SAT at Jesus' feet, Martha busily made preparations to serve Jesus (see Luke 10:39-40). But Martha forgot what Mary knew: being with Jesus is the only thing worth being concerned about.

If we're not putting Jesus first in all our efforts, then we are striving in vain. We must first seek him and worship him—and *then* good works will follow. Busyness is not a virtue. God did not design us to sprint from one crisis to the next. He designed us to sit at the feet of Christ.

A woman who lives with the stress of an
overwhelmed schedule will often ache with
the sadness of an underwhelmed soul.

LYSA TERKEURST

ALL AUTHORITY

*I have been given all authority
in heaven and on earth.*

MATTHEW 28:18

ALL AUTHORITY. Nothing in the universe is more powerful than Jesus. There is absolutely nothing that does not fall under his command—not Satan, not solar systems, not nations, not governments, not presidents, not sin, not addiction, not earthquakes, not diseases, *not one thing.* Anyone or anything that tries to challenge his authority will once and for all be defeated.

That means we have nothing to fear, because everything is subject to the one we voluntarily serve. It's good to be on his side! Jesus has authority over our lives and our deaths, and he chose to abolish death for us and replace it with eternal life by his side. Thank you, Jesus!

The dominion of Death is blown to bits on Easter Day.
FLEMING RUTLEDGE

No Dark Corners

*If you are filled with light, with no dark corners,
then your whole life will be radiant, as though
a floodlight were filling you with light.*

LUKE 11:36

"NO DARK CORNERS." Well, that's not going to be easy. Most of us have something lingering in the back, just out of sight, some pocket of pain or hate or fear.

But Jesus wants to flood our lives with his light, casting out every last speck of darkness. Then our lives will be radiant. Then we will be able to meet others where they are and say, "Hey, do you want to have a radiant life too?" Then we can help shine Jesus' light into their dark corners.

*Let God send you in a new direction today. Meet
someone at the crossroads of his or her life. Put
on a bright face whether you feel like it or not.*

JUNE MASTERS BACHER

HYPOCRITES!

You Pharisees are so careful to clean the outside of the cup and the dish, but inside you are filthy—full of greed and wickedness! Fools! Didn't God make the inside as well as the outside? So clean the inside by giving gifts to the poor, and you will be clean all over.

LUKE 11:39-41

WHAT A POWERFUL way to describe the hypocrisy that still plagues the church today. When we act like shiny, plastic people but do not seek God with our hearts, we are really missing the boat.

If we live like this, people will look at us and see anything but Jesus. We must live in grace—honestly and authentically—if people are going to see Jesus in us.

If you keep your eyes on Christians, you will be disappointed every day of your life. Your hope is to keep your eyes on Christ.

JAN KARON

SNEAKY

Beware! Guard against every kind of greed.
Life is not measured by how much you own.

LUKE 12:15

GREED IS SNEAKY. You may think you're not greedy, but then you see someone with a new car and think, "How did they afford *that*?" Or your nephew enters the gifted and talented program, and you are resentful because your child is struggling in school.

Greed can get its claws into you even if you're not a materialistic money-lover, because greed sneaks into spots where contentment should be. If you're unsatisfied with your current rust bucket, greed sneaks in. If you're ungrateful for this season with your children, greed sneaks in.

Good thing contentment drives out greed. "Thank you, Jesus, that this car just started." "Thank you, Jesus, that my son can read." "Thank you, Jesus, for everything."

With God, it's possible to be content wherever
we are, with whatever we have.

TRICIA GOYER

REAL RICHES

*Yes, a person is a fool to store up earthly wealth
but not have a rich relationship with God.*

LUKE 12:21

JESUS CALLING someone a fool seems pretty harsh. But
he's not wrong, obviously. After all, how foolish is it to
put all our resources (time, energy, money) into something we can't take with us?

Do we really *need* that new ATV, that bigger house, that
fancy car, that promotion, that endorsement, that title? Do
we *need* our kids to be the best at that musical instrument or
sport? Do we *need* to pour so much time into that hobby?
Will any of that matter when we're in heaven?

*Don't put all your hope and faith into something that
could suddenly and easily disappear. And honestly,
that's almost anything. The only thing that will never
go away, that will never fail you, is your faith in God.*

BETHANY HAMILTON

LET THE CHILDREN COME

*Let the children come to me. Don't stop
them! For the Kingdom of Heaven belongs
to those who are like these children.*

MATTHEW 19:14

THE MANY PAINTINGS that depict Jesus surrounded by children are probably fairly accurate. They probably really did crawl all over him, loving on him and being loved. They may have even pulled his beard.

Jesus loved children. And so should we. Whether we have children of our own or not, we can recognize how precious they are, with their vitality, their innocence, and their thirst for knowledge. As grown-ups, it is our job to love, protect, and disciple these children.

And perhaps the best thing we can do for children is pray for them. Do you know a child you could pray for today?

*The soul of a child is the loveliest flower
That grows in the garden of God.*

AUTHOR UNKNOWN

WHERE IS YOUR TREASURE?

*Wherever your treasure is, there the
desires of your heart will also be.*

LUKE 12:34

WE INVEST our energies into the things we think are most
important. If we prioritize things like money, success, and
what other people think of us, we will reap things like
anxiety, disappointment, and grief. But if we recognize
that our treasure lies in Jesus, we will reap joy, contentment, and blessings.

There is only one kind of treasure that really matters,
only one kind of treasure that satisfies: a relationship with
Jesus. Invest your energy in that today, and live your day
to the fullest.

*The spiritual man and woman can afford to take
desperate chances, and live dangerously in the
interests of their ideals; being delivered from the
many unreal fears and anxieties which commonly
torment us, and knowing the unimportance
of possessions and of so-called success.*

EVELYN UNDERHILL

JESUS' BANQUET

When you put on a luncheon or a banquet . . .
don't invite your friends, brothers, relatives, and
rich neighbors. . . . Instead, invite the poor, the
crippled, the lame, and the blind. Then at the
resurrection of the righteous, God will reward
you for inviting those who could not repay you.

LUKE 14:12-14

WE WILL NOT ALWAYS be comfortable ministering to those Jesus calls us to minister to. He will call us to love people with different worldviews, different lifestyles, and different incomes.

Our comfort levels are not the point. Jesus has called us to minister to the poor, the messy, the lost. And when we do, we will be rewarded.

When you offer peace instead of division,
faith instead of fear, when you offer someone
a place at your table instead of keeping them
out because they're different or messy or wrong
somehow, you represent the heart of Christ.

SHAUNA NIEQUIST

THE LOST COIN

*Suppose a woman has ten silver coins and
loses one. Won't she light a lamp and sweep
the entire house and search carefully until she
finds it? And when she finds it, she will call in
her friends and neighbors and say, "Rejoice
with me because I have found my lost coin."*

LUKE 15:8-9

IN THIS PARABLE, the lost coin represents a sinner who
comes to Jesus. Can you imagine? Someone who was lost
cries out to Jesus, and heaven erupts in celebration! If
Jesus said it, this is how it really is.

This rejoicing and celebrating happened when you
chose Jesus too. And it's what happens when all those seeds
you've planted and watered in others come to fruition.

*Maybe you have escaped God. One adventure took
you to the next and suddenly you were lost in a
crowd, wondering if you'd gone too far. You haven't.
Stop. Right where you are. Let Him scoop you up.*

SUZIE ELLER

THE PRODIGAL SON

We had to celebrate this happy day. For
your brother was dead and has come back
to life! He was lost, but now he is found!

LUKE 15:32

THROUGH THE PARABLE of the Prodigal Son, Jesus taught that it's never too late to come home to God, our Father. Though we may wander away from him, as long as we are breathing, we still have a chance to run to God's open arms, where we will be received with joy and excitement.

You may know someone who is lost or who is living the prodigal lifestyle, but it is never too late for this precious son or daughter. Keep praying for that soul, and trust Jesus to do what he does best: save his sheep.

Love loosed a wind of words: "My son is coming home."

MAURA EICHNER

FAITHFUL IN LITTLE THINGS

If you are faithful in little things, you will be faithful in large ones. But if you are dishonest in little things, you won't be honest with greater responsibilities.

LUKE 16:10

IF GOD CAN'T TRUST us with the little things, he's not going to give us big things to accomplish. So we can prepare ourselves to do "big things" for God by making sure we are honest in the small things, the things we sometimes think don't matter.

How did you respond to that driver who cut you off? What did you do when the server accidentally charged you much less than what your lunch cost? What did you do with the parking ticket from the town you'll never visit again? God sees these things, so they matter.

Choosing to live without a shadow of dishonesty will establish you as a trustworthy woman before God and others.

GLYNNIS WHITWER

THE HEALING THAT MATTERS

Jesus asked, "Didn't I heal ten men? . . . Has no one returned to give glory to God except this foreigner?" And Jesus said to the man, "Stand up and go. Your faith has healed you."

LUKE 17:17-19

TEN MEN CRIED out to Jesus, "Heal us!" So Jesus healed them of their leprosy. But only one came running back to Jesus, shouting, "Praise God!" (see Luke 17:12-15). And to that man, Jesus said, "Your faith has healed you."

Look at what the other nine missed out on—the spiritual healing they so desperately needed. It's a sad story—but not for the man who did return, did bow, did worship. That man will be with Jesus forever.

Being truly thank-full requires looking beyond our blessings, to the One who blesses. It's about being full of gratitude for Christ, not just being full of thanks for what He has given us or done.

TRACIE MILES

THE KINGDOM IS NOW

The Kingdom of God can't be detected
by visible signs. You won't be able to say,
"Here it is!" or "It's over there!" For the
Kingdom of God is already among you.

LUKE 17:20-21

THE PHARISEES EXPECTED a Messiah who would arrive
with a splash, one who would wipe out Roman rule and
set up his own physical throne in its place. As we know,
this did not happen, because God had something much
bigger planned—a kingdom we can all be a part of, one
that includes the spiritual realm. His Kingdom is here
both now and forever. His Kingdom is one we can live
in for eternity as citizens.

The Kingdom of God is here.
We're alive for something eternal.

KARI JOBE, MIA FIELDES, AND PAUL BALOCHE

HUMBLED OR EXALTED?

Those who exalt themselves will be humbled, and those who humble themselves will be exalted.

LUKE 18:14

JESUS WARNED US against trying to exalt ourselves, but he also encouraged those who humble themselves that they will be exalted. The difficulty comes when we take pride in our humility. When this happens, we can immediately ask for forgiveness. A contrite heart is a humble heart.

So many times we find ourselves in humbling situations, but we can trust in the fact that our circumstances are trivial in God's big picture. No matter how humbling this life on earth is, we belong to the one true King who will exalt us, in God's timing, so that he may be glorified.

Whenever we are sure that we are among the righteous, we immediately find ourselves among the arrogant.

FLEMING RUTLEDGE

GIVE

Sell all your possessions and give the money to the poor, and you will have treasure in heaven.

LUKE 18:22

JESUS TOLD THE RICH religious leader to sell everything he had. In the same way, if Jesus asks us to give something up, we need to say yes. If Jesus asks us to give something away, we need to say yes. If he asks us to sell something so we can have money to help someone else, we need to say yes.

How can we be so willing? By recognizing that nothing we own is really ours in the first place. It *all* came from God: our possessions, our money, our talents, and even our time. These things are just entrusted to us so we can use them to accomplish the work of God.

The only way to prevent our possessions from possessing us, is to develop a habit of generosity.

SHARON HODDE MILLER

 APRIL 21

HOSPITALITY

*Quick, come down! I must be a
guest in your home today.*

LUKE 19:5

ZACCHAEUS WAS A CHIEF tax collector who had cheated
poor people out of money (see Luke 19:2)—and yet Jesus
said he was going to come visit. Surely Zacchaeus did not
expect Jesus to want to come to his home. Most likely,
he did not think himself worthy of such a guest. But he
opened his home to Jesus anyway.

So many women think their home is not big enough,
clean enough, or nice enough to welcome guests. But this
is a lie. We never know when God wants us to invite someone in, and it is the attitude of the person in the home that
makes a home welcoming, not the home itself. Whom can
you welcome, in the name of Jesus, into your home today?

*The heart of hospitality is about creating space
for someone to feel seen and heard and loved.*

SHAUNA NIEQUIST

DON'T PANIC

When you hear of wars and insurrections,
don't panic. Yes, these things must take place
first, but the end won't follow immediately.

LUKE 21:9

OUR WORLD IS WAR TORN. Just watching the news can cause us to panic. But Jesus said, "Don't panic." The Bible tells us the end of the story: Jesus wins. Yes, our world will go through much turmoil until we reach that end, but it is ultimately his victory that matters. So when we find ourselves frightened, anxious, and grieving about the state of things, we can turn to our Savior and say, "Thank you for winning this war. Help me to be patient as the details play out."

God is in control. He always has been, and he will be through the end of this world. Aren't you glad you're on his side?

Let nothing disturb you,
Let nothing frighten you,
All things are passing away:
God never changes.

TERESA OF AVILA

PERSECUTION FOR A PURPOSE

There will be a time of great persecution. . . . But this will be your opportunity to tell them about me.

LUKE 21:12-13

NONE OF US DESIRE to be persecuted, but most of us will experience persecution when we follow Jesus. The inspiring news is that this suffering isn't in vain. When we are persecuted, we have opportunities to show others the grace of Christ.

Our suffering will be short lived. But if our suffering leads someone to Jesus, then that will lead to ceaseless joy.

> *In the greatest of our afflictions we could not say in our hearts, "Father, would thou hadst not brought us here!" but cried mightily to our God for power to carry us through whatsoever should be inflicted upon us, that the Truth of our God might not suffer through our weakness.*

KATHARINE EVANS

STAND FIRM

Not a hair of your head will perish! By standing firm, you will win your souls.

LUKE 21:18-19

JESUS TAUGHT his disciples about the end of the world as they knew it, and he told them that some pretty scary stuff was coming: wars, earthquakes, famines, plagues, great persecution. They must have been terrified. But then he told them that they wouldn't lose a single hair on their heads. He told them to stand firm.

He tells us the same thing. We are living in perilous times. There are natural disasters and terminal illnesses and crimes we don't even want to think about, but we have Jesus protecting us. All we need to do is stand firm, persevere, trust Jesus, and love one another in the meantime.

Stay calm.
Trust Me.
In patience you possess your soul.

MARIE CHAPIAN

THIS IS MY BODY

[Jesus] took some bread and gave thanks to God
for it. Then he broke it in pieces and gave it to
the disciples, saying, "This is my body, which is
given for you. Do this in remembrance of me."

LUKE 22:19

JESUS GAVE his body for *you*. Communion is one way for us to remember and thank him for this miraculous gift.

Let us not fall prey to thinking of Communion as nothing but a routine. It is not an empty act of ritual. It is a loving act of obedience, a way to connect with Jesus in a personal and holy way. It's not just something we do every week or every month; it's something that can profoundly change our hearts for the better.

The heart preparing for Communion should be
as a crystal vial filled with clear water in which
the least mote of uncleanness will be seen.

ELIZABETH SETON

THIS CUP OF SUFFERING

*Father, if you are willing, please take
this cup of suffering away from me. Yet
I want your will to be done, not mine.*

LUKE 22:42

JESUS KNEW he would suffer. In his humanness, he asked his Father to prevent the suffering if it was according to his will.

But God did not.

After Jesus surrendered to God's will, an angel from heaven came to strengthen Jesus (see Luke 22:43).

We will experience grief. But God's will is a protective umbrella over all of it. We can talk to him during our suffering, and even if he answers, "You must endure this," we can be certain he will enable us to do so.

*Through God's grace, he gives us a wealth of resources
to bear any burden he allows. Therefore, if God doesn't
empty our cup of suffering or take it from us, he will
give ample grace (favor, kindness, ability) to bear it.*

JENNIFER ROTHSCHILD

THEY DON'T KNOW WHAT THEY ARE DOING

Father, forgive them, for they don't know what they are doing.

LUKE 23:34

THEY DIDN'T KNOW what they were doing. They didn't know they were crucifying the Son of God. They didn't know they were helping to bring about the most important moment in history.

And through his suffering, Jesus did not look down on them with bitterness, scorn, anger, or condescension. No, he called out to his Father on their behalf.

Sometimes, we don't even know we are sinning. Sometimes, we *do* know we are sinning, but we don't understand just how grave our offenses are. And still, Jesus intercedes for us. Jesus is interceding for you right now (see Romans 8:34).

Down from his cross poured redemptive love in quantity enough for the whole human race. Enough for you.

EUGENIA PRICE

THE CHOICE

I assure you, today you will be with me in paradise.

LUKE 23:43

JESUS' CROSS STOOD with two others. He was crucified alongside two criminals, who represent for us all sinners who have ever lived. Every sinner has a choice: she can scoff, or she can fear God. To the sinner on the cross who chose to fear God, Jesus promised paradise.

If you have chosen to fear God, it means you have chosen Jesus, the only way *to* God, and you will be with Jesus one day in paradise. Jesus died on that cross to make an eternity with him a reality for you—and for the men, women, and children you will meet today. Each one of them has a choice. Will you help them make it?

Jesus would have died for one person, for one sinner.

MOTHER TERESA

A GIFT

Jesus shouted, "Father, I entrust my spirit into your hands!" And with those words he breathed his last.

LUKE 23:46

THE ROMANS WEREN'T in charge. Neither were the Jews. Jesus was.

Jesus willingly gave up his life. For you. This was a gift, a voluntary sacrifice. He knew it was God's will, and he chose to obey God even though it meant his suffering and death.

But Jesus knew his spirit was going into God's hands and that he would be returning to paradise. And thanks to Jesus' voluntary gift, we don't need to fear suffering or death. We have comfort in knowing that when it is our time to leave this earth, our spirits will be held in God's eternal, capable hands.

At the cross I bow my knee,
Where Your blood was shed for me.
There's no greater love than this.

DARLENE ZSCHECH

JESUS LOVES YOU

This is how God loved the world: He gave his
one and only Son, so that everyone who believes
in him will not perish but have eternal life.

JOHN 3:16

JESUS LOVES YOU. In all the crazy busyness of life, it can
be easy to forget this. Sometimes you just need to stop
what you're doing and meditate on this fact: Jesus loves
you.

He loved you enough to leave paradise and come to
this broken world of dust and stink and pain. He loved
you enough to suffer at the hands of foolish men. He
loved you enough to die.

Jesus' love is beyond anything we can comprehend,
and yet, we get to live in this love. We don't have to
understand something to live in its reality.

You are loved, you are beautiful, you are treasured,
and you are a daughter of the living God.

SHEILA WALSH

THE WOMAN AT THE WELL

*If you only knew the gift God has for you
and who you are speaking to, you would ask
me, and I would give you living water.*

JOHN 4:10

THIS VERSE IS PART of the longest conversation recorded between Jesus and any one person in the Bible (see John 4:6-30). And it's with a woman—a Samaritan woman, whom most Jewish men in those days would have avoided. So she is understandably baffled when Jesus begins the conversation by asking her for a drink. She responds, "Why are you even talking to me?"

But Jesus chose to speak to her, and by sharing his truth with her, her entire village learned about the Messiah. This wasn't an accident. Jesus sees men and women the same: through eyes of love (see Galatians 3:28).

Women matter to Jesus. You matter to Jesus.

*You are women, and a woman is
always a beautiful thing.*

JOSEPHINE BUTLER

SECRETS

You're right! You don't have a husband—for you
have had five husbands, and you aren't even
married to the man you're living with now.

JOHN 4:17-18

GREAT NEWS: Jesus knows all your dark secrets, just as he knew the Samaritan woman's. Why is this great news? Because you don't have to invest any energy in trying to hide them from him. He not only knows them but also will *use* them to mold you into the person he wants you to be. Dark seasons are only building blocks toward the light.

Our past is what brings us to our future. When I pray
for someone, I thank God for every day of their life,
for every moment, for every heartbreak and each
moment of happiness that has brought them to be this
person at this time. I believe in mining through the
darkest seasons in our lives and choosing to believe
that we'll find something important every time.

SHAUNA NIEQUIST

IN SPIRIT AND TRUTH

God is Spirit, so those who worship him
must worship in spirit and in truth.

JOHN 4:24

JESUS WANTS TO SET us free from ritualistic worship. While some of us may still take comfort in spiritual routines, it is the spirit of our worship—not the routine—that matters. We must worship God with our spirits (not just our bodies, voices, or minds), and we must worship in truth. If we're just going through the motions, without meaning, then it just doesn't count.

Worshiping God with our spirits brings tremendous blessings. In doing so, we enter into a genuine, living relationship with him, and we can trust in his care for us.

No form of worship, however sacred, is regarded as
established, only so far as it expresses the gift and
leading of the Spirit. . . . The life of the spirit, not
the form of expression, is regarded as essential.

ATTRIBUTED TO ANNA WHITE

TRUE NOURISHMENT

*My nourishment comes from doing the will of
God, who sent me, and from finishing his work.*

JOHN 4:34

WOMEN OFTEN TRY to fill themselves with things other
than God. They might try sex, drugs, alcohol, or gam-
bling, or even something that seems more innocent:
romance, wealth, a nice home, friendships, a career, or
children. But even the best things in this life won't fill us
up in the end.

The only way we're going to be really nourished is by
God and, according to Jesus, by doing God's will. So the
next time you feel like you're running on empty, ask God,
"What do you want me to do today?" Then walk in his
will and feel your tank fill to overflowing.

*There is nothing quite so fulfilling as
completing an assignment for God.*

JILL BRISCOE

ABUNDANCE

After everyone was full, Jesus told his disciples, "Now gather the leftovers, so that nothing is wasted."

JOHN 6:12

MORE THAN FIVE THOUSAND people sat on the hillside listening to Jesus. He didn't have a microphone—or a caterer. He did have a boy with five loaves of bread and two fish, and some disciples who didn't yet understand what Jesus could do (see John 6:8-11).

Jesus broke the bread and passed it around. Not only did no one leave hungry, but everyone was *full*—and there were *leftovers*!

When God blesses us, he does it abundantly. If you're living with abundance right now, don't let it be wasted. How can you use those leftover miracles today?

Perhaps the Lord allows us to have more than our portion as an opportunity for us to share the good things we have with others who are in need.

CRYSTAL MCDOWELL

BREAD OF LIFE

*I am the bread of life. Whoever comes to
me will never be hungry again. Whoever
believes in me will never be thirsty.*

JOHN 6:35

JESUS IS THE BREAD OF LIFE—essential to our spiritual nourishment. We can sometimes fall into a pattern of thinking of Jesus as "up there" or "in the Bible," forgetting that he is also right here with us, as real as any tangible thing. When we keep Jesus in our daily lives, as a Savior and friend who is right here by our side, he will feed the hunger of our souls. He is concrete, absolute, and necessary—every single day.

*Break thou the bread of life, dear Lord, to me,
As thou didst break the loaves beside the sea;
Beyond the sacred page I seek thee, Lord;
My spirit pants for thee, O Living Word!*

MARY ARTEMISIA LATHBURY

NOT MY OWN WILL

I have come down from heaven to do the will
of God who sent me, not to do my own will.

JOHN 6:38

JESUS' INTENT WAS to do the will of God, even when it included his own death. Are we willing to do the same? There will always be some tension between what we want and what God wants, but when we consistently choose what God wants, we live within his will.

Living within God's will leads to blessings that include peace of mind and a contented heart. We may think we know what we want and the best way to get it, but unless our ideas align with God's, we are wrong. We would do well to follow Jesus' example and choose to do God's will.

The center of God's will is our only safety.
BETSIE TEN BOOM

SIMPLE

*It is my Father's will that all who see his
Son and believe in him should have eternal
life. I will raise them up at the last day.*

JOHN 6:40

WHAT PURELY ENCOURAGING words, straight from Jesus'
lips. It is God's will (the God who *created* you) that once
you see and believe in Jesus, you will live forever. And
Jesus *himself* will be the one to raise you from the dead!

We can take this fantastic news to others. This is a
great verse to share with someone who is just being intro-
duced to Jesus. Salvation really can be a simple affair:
Jesus died to make it accessible to every one of us.

*The Lord Jesus characterizes the simplicity
and certainty of saving faith, stating that
it is his Father's will to grant eternal life to
all who look on and believe in him.*

ELYSE M. FITZPATRICK

THE VOID

The Spirit alone gives eternal life. Human effort
accomplishes nothing. And the very words
I have spoken to you are spirit and life.

JOHN 6:63

WE HUMANS ARE GOOD at striving. We build the smartest computers, the tallest buildings, and the fastest cars. We create works of art: epic poems, paintings, sculptures, and fashionable clothes. And we women love to plan things: showers, weddings, vacations, and church programs.

But what does it all amount to apart from Jesus? Nothing. What can we even accomplish apart from Jesus? Nothing. All around you people are coming to this realization, this emptiness. Whether or not they're ready to admit it to you, people are sensing the void that can be filled only by Jesus.

He is so big . . . and we are so nothing.
ANNE GRAHAM LOTZ

ALL WHO ARE THIRSTY

Anyone who is thirsty may come to me!
Anyone who believes in me may come and
drink! For the Scriptures declare, "Rivers of
living water will flow from his heart."

JOHN 7:37-38

THESE BELOVED WORDS of Jesus provide a poetic summation of the gospel. If someone is *thirsty*, they can *come*, *believe*, and *drink*. First, someone must acknowledge their thirst. Then they must believe in Jesus. Then they must come to him, as he doesn't force his living water on anyone. And then they get to drink the living water (receive the Holy Spirit).

The quenching they receive is so powerful that it changes their lives forever. The Holy Spirit will never leave them, and they will never thirst again.

Come to God with your emptiness, and
He will fill you with His best!

ALISA HOPE WAGNER

THE LIGHT THAT LEADS TO LIFE

*I am the light of the world. If you follow me,
you won't have to walk in darkness, because
you will have the light that leads to life.*

JOHN 8:12

NOTHING GOOD HAPPENS in the darkness. People get lost.
Fears are born. Promises are broken. Crimes are executed.
Violence is committed. Traps are set. People run into
walls and trip over obstacles they can't see. People take
advantage of others. It is the opposite of Kingdom life.

But if we follow Jesus, we don't have to walk in the
darkness. We can stay in the light—the safe, beautiful,
wholesome light that leads to life here and now and to
life eternal.

*Today the approaching kingdoms of darkness
and light are clearer than ever before.
They are taking shape here on earth.*

BASILEA SCHLINK

THE ONLY WAY TO FREEDOM

*You will know the truth, and the
truth will set you free.*

JOHN 8:32

AS LITTLE GIRLS, many of us were taught the lie that a great career meant a great life. Many of us believed in fairy tales—that the perfect romance would lead to a happily ever after. And some of us invested our hope in talents; we wanted to be ballerinas, pianists, and Olympians. We thought these things would give us joy in life.

But they don't. The truth is that no matter which goal we choose, they all lead to the same end: a place of longing for the only thing that can truly satisfy us and free us to enjoy life. And that thing is a personal relationship with the King of the universe, Jesus Christ.

*Beloved, whatever we are gripping to bring
us satisfaction is a lie—unless it is Christ.
He is the Truth that sets us free.*

BETH MOORE

TRULY FREE

If the Son sets you free, you are truly free.

JOHN 8:36

ONCE JESUS SETS you free from sin, you are free for eternity. You will still have to battle temptation, work to break habits, and maybe even fight against addiction, but Jesus has already beaten sin for you. All you have to do is live in him and walk in your freedom.

Nothing can put the shackles and chains back on you. You are victorious. You are heaven bound. You are free of death, free of sin, free of hopelessness, free of loneliness. You are free to serve Jesus, free to serve others, free to make this world a better place, free to help Jesus' Kingdom grow. Truly free. And no one can take that away from you.

*The traps of the past are shattered
and done away with.*

MARIE CHAPIAN

FORGIVE OTHERS, FREE YOURSELF

*If you refuse to forgive others, your
Father will not forgive your sins.*

MATTHEW 6:15

MAKE NO MISTAKE. Jesus knows how difficult it is for us to forgive people who have hurt us and those who will readily hurt us again. He's not teaching that forgiveness is easy; he's teaching that it's necessary.

But he doesn't say this in order to punish us. Sometimes it feels satisfying to hold on to some unforgiveness, but that is not healthy for us. Jesus tells us to forgive, because by forgiving others, our own hearts are released from a prison of bitterness.

If you are having trouble forgiving someone, know that Jesus has already been through this struggle. Ask him to help you forgive the person who has hurt you. Ask him to set your heart free.

*He who cannot forgive others, breaks the
bridge over which he himself must pass.*

CORRIE TEN BOOM

I AM

I tell you the truth, before Abraham
was even born, I AM!

JOHN 8:58

CHANGE ISN'T ALWAYS EASY. Life is hard, in part because of the constant changes. We change jobs, sometimes even careers. Our children grow up. People move away. We move away. Loved ones go to heaven, and we have to learn to live without them.

It seems we are always having to adjust or adapt, just to keep moving ahead. As we struggle with all these bumps, hills, and sharp curves, we can take comfort in the fact that Jesus has been the same since before time began, and he will be the same into eternity. He doesn't change. He is our constant.

Behold Him there the risen Lamb,
My perfect spotless righteousness,
The great unchangeable I AM,
The King of glory and of grace,
One with Himself I cannot die.

CHARITIE L. BANCROFT

FOR THE GLORY OF GOD

*"It was not because of his sins or his parents'
sins," Jesus answered. "This happened so
the power of God could be seen in him."*

JOHN 9:3

THE DISCIPLES WANTED to know why a man on the street
was blind. Was it because of his sins? Or his parents' sins?
(See John 9:1-2.) And Jesus said, "Neither." Notice he
didn't say, "They didn't sin." He just said, "That's not
the point."

The point was that this man's blindness would show
others God's glory.

Our struggles can also be used to glorify God. We
shouldn't waste time overanalyzing which circumstances
are the result of which sins. We just need to say to God,
"Use me, God—*all* of me, even my brokenness and
ugliness—for your glory." And he will.

*Stripping away the sheath of self,
this is how we see God.*

ANN VOSKAMP

THE LIGHT OF THE WORLD

*While I am here in the world, I am
the light of the world.*

JOHN 9:5

THE LIGHT OF THE WORLD. It doesn't get much more inspiring than that. The longer we live this life, the better we understand just how dark this world is. But when Jesus showed up in human form, it changed everything. He was a miraculous beam of light that shone for miles around, changing the entire landscape of the world.

He is no longer here in human form. But he is still here. He is here in spirit, and he is here in you. He is still the only light in a dark, suffering world, and we can cling to that light with all our might.

*How wonderful that the reality of his presence
is greater than the reality of the hell about us.*

BETSIE TEN BOOM

A RICH AND SATISFYING LIFE

*The thief's purpose is to steal and kill and destroy.
My purpose is to give them a rich and satisfying life.*

JOHN 10:10

SATAN DOESN'T WANT Jesus, the Good Shepherd, to have
healthy, happy sheep. Satan doesn't want us living richly
or contentedly. Satan wants us spiritually dead. But Jesus
isn't going to allow that, because we are *his* sheep. Instead
of death, Jesus gives us abundant life—now and forever!

How do we receive that gift? We need to abide in
Jesus. We need to remain in his protection, obey his commands, and follow his teachings. When we abide in Jesus,
life is full of richness and satisfaction.

*As Christians we find it easy to wonder where
abundant life is.... This is right where Satan
wants us—believing in some of the truth but not
fully convinced that Christ himself is the truth.*

DEBBIE ALSDORF

THE GOOD SHEPHERD

*I am the good shepherd. The good shepherd
sacrifices his life for the sheep.*

JOHN 10:11

IT'S DIFFICULT FOR our twenty-first-century selves to picture the first-century shepherd who devoted his every waking moment to the care of the sheep. He was their protector, their guardian, their provider, their everything.

A good shepherd would even value the life of his sheep over his own. This is what Jesus did for us. Imagine if we truly were sheep. Imagine how unlikely it would seem for a mighty king to sacrifice his life to save an insignificant animal. Yet that is what Jesus did. The God of the universe died for mere sheep—for you and me.

*Wherever He may guide me,
No want shall turn me back;
My Shepherd is beside me,
And nothing can I lack.*

ANNA L. WARING

ALL WE CAN DO

Because you have obeyed my command to
persevere, I will protect you from the great
time of testing that will come upon the whole
world to test those who belong to this world.

REVELATION 3:10

JESUS SPOKE COMFORTING words to the church in
Philadelphia, often called the Faithful Church. Jesus
commended these people for their obedience and perseverance, and he made them a promise: he would protect
them from a time of great testing that will come upon
the world.

We don't know exactly what the future holds. But
Jesus tells us that the world's situation will get worse
before it gets better. All we can do is be faithful and persevere, trusting Jesus to protect us.

Let us then be true and faithful,
Trusting, serving every day;
Just one glimpse of Him in glory
Will the toils of life repay.

ELIZA E. HEWITT

IN GOD'S TIMING

*Lazarus's sickness will not end in death. No,
it happened for the glory of God so that the
Son of God will receive glory from this.*

JOHN 11:4

WHEN LAZARUS GOT SICK, his sisters, Mary and Martha,
sent for Jesus. But Jesus didn't respond as they expected.
Instead of rushing to Lazarus's side, he said, "It'll be all
right." Then he took his time about coming (see John
11:1-7).

Often we ask Jesus for something and expect him to
come running to save the day. When he doesn't, we wonder why. It's so easy to forget that he sees into the future.
He sees what we *really* need, and he is eager to provide it
for us! And what he does provide will be bigger and better
than what we asked for in the first place.

*Often God delays purposely, and the delay
is just as much an answer to your prayer
as is the fulfillment when it comes.*

L. B. E. COWMAN

HE IS THE RESURRECTION

*I am the resurrection and the life. Anyone who
believes in me will live, even after dying. Everyone
who lives in me and believes in me will never ever die.*

JOHN 11:25-26

JESUS CAME TO SEE Mary and Martha after their brother,
Lazarus, had died. Jesus spoke these words to Martha
just before he raised Lazarus from the grave. Martha was
grieving, but through her grief, she knew Jesus was capable of anything (see John 11:17-22).

Jesus specializes in resurrection. He resurrects
friendships, marriages, careers, and finances. He is able
to breathe new life into anyone or anything. We love
and worship the very same Jesus as Mary, Martha, and
Lazarus did. What needs resurrecting in your life?

> *God's specialty is raising dead things to life
> and making impossible things possible. You
> don't have the need that exceeds His power.*
>
> BETH MOORE

WHERE CREDIT IS DUE

They rolled the stone aside. Then Jesus looked up to heaven and said, "Father, thank you for hearing me."

JOHN 11:41

AS FAR AS WE KNOW from Scripture, Jesus didn't audibly thank God before every miracle, but he did it at Lazarus's tomb so that all the people who were watching would know that God was responsible for the miracle they were about to witness—a resurrection.

We can benefit from following Jesus' example in this situation. When we thank God for the blessings he is about to give us, we show people (family, friends, coworkers, Christian brothers and sisters) to whom the credit belongs. We don't have to make a big show of our gratitude, but we can humbly make sure that the people around us know that miracles are not luck but blessings from heaven.

*Eucharisteo—thanksgiving—
always precedes the miracle.*

ANN VOSKAMP

LIFE IN THIS WORLD

Those who love their life in this world will lose it. Those who care nothing for their life in this world will keep it for eternity.

JOHN 12:25

THERE ARE A LOT of things about this life to love, cherish, and enjoy. We love our families. We love our homes. Some of us love our jobs or our ministries. We love our friends. We love our hobbies and pastimes. We enjoy good books, sweet movies, and engrossing television shows. We enjoy chocolate cake and popcorn.

But none of these things compare to our Savior. And when we put any of these things ahead of him, we are losing out on the best thing of all: the opportunity to worship him above all else.

God has a lot more to give and to offer than the world has to give.

BETHANY HAMILTON

CHILD OF THE LIGHT

Put your trust in the light while there is still time;
then you will become children of the light.

JOHN 12:36

WHEN WE PUT our trust in God's light, that light burns away all the darkness in our soul. The love of Jesus transforms us into children of the light, God's pure children, the saints who make up the body of Christ.

As children of the light, we get to walk in love and truth, free of dark traits such as fear, hatred, and shame. You are a child of the light! May you shine brightly today, unencumbered by the darkness of this world.

A saint is a human creature devoured and
transformed by love: a love that has dissolved
and burnt out those instinctive passions—
acquisitive and combative, proud and greedy—
which commonly rule the lives of men.

EVELYN UNDERHILL

TRUST HIM IN EVERYTHING

*If you trust me, you are trusting not only
me, but also God who sent me.*

JOHN 12:44

THERE ARE COUNTLESS levels of trusting Jesus. We trust
him for our salvation. As we read, study, and learn his
Word, we trust him that what he says is true. We trust
him with our prayer requests. We trust him with our
relationships, with our finances, with our children's and
grandchildren's futures.

Is there any area of your life where trust is lacking?
One sure way to tell is to look for fear. If you find fear in
your life, then that's an area where you are not trusting
Jesus. Give your fear to Jesus, and be free of it.

*The fear is suffocating, terrorizing, and I want
the remedy, and it is trust. Trust is everything.*

ANN VOSKAMP

YOU DON'T UNDERSTAND

*You don't understand now what I am
doing, but someday you will.*

JOHN 13:7

CAN YOU EVEN IMAGINE watching Jesus, the King of the universe, kneeling in front of you to wash your feet? When he did so for the disciples, Peter objected, horrified. He didn't understand that Jesus washed his disciples' tired, filthy feet to demonstrate humility (see John 13:4-16).

We often don't understand the meaning of things when they are happening. But we need to trust that Jesus knows what he is doing. He's probably trying to teach us something. Who are we to argue? And, as Jesus told Peter, someday we will understand—maybe in this life, maybe in the next.

*He does not discuss things with us. He
leads us faithfully and plainly as we trust
Him and simply do the next thing.*

ELISABETH ELLIOT

LOVE EACH OTHER

I am giving you a new commandment:
Love each other. Just as I have loved
you, you should love each other.

JOHN 13:34

WHEN JESUS FIRST gave this command to his disciples, it
may have seemed simple to them. *Love each other? That's*
it? But it's harder than it sounds, isn't it? In a world so
steeped in darkness, overwhelming need, pain, and suffering, how do we even make a dent?

One person at a time. Whom can you love today?
Whom can you listen to today? Whom can you bring
food to today? Whom can you hug today? When you
do these things, you are obeying Jesus' commandment.

Love is born when we misunderstand one another
and make it right, when we cry in the kitchen,
when we show up uninvited with magazines and
granola bars, in an effort to say, I love you.

SHAUNA NIEQUIST

LAST PLACE

Whoever wants to be first must take last place and be the servant of everyone else.

MARK 9:35

WE MAY LIVE in a dog-eat-dog world, but God's realm isn't a dog-eat-dog Kingdom. If we want to finish first in God's system, we must put ourselves last—in other words, live entirely counter to the surrounding culture.

This would be impossible if it weren't for the miraculous power of the Holy Spirit living within us. But as we practice, serving others gets easier, because we can see God working through our servanthood.

If we look for opportunities to serve others and put their needs ahead of our own, if we never consider ourselves above doing tasks that seem menial, if we build others up instead of ourselves—that's when we're on the track to greatness in God's eyes. And we just might discover that last place is the best place to be after all.

DIANNE NEAL MATTHEWS

DON'T LET YOUR HEARTS BE TROUBLED

*Don't let your hearts be troubled. Trust
in God, and trust also in me.*

JOHN 14:1

ONE OF THE MOST DIFFICULT things to give up to God
is a broken heart. A broken heart is so personal. It is so
real. How can we give something up that is so deeply a
part of ourselves?

And yet, that's what Jesus is telling us to do. He
doesn't want us to live with troubled hearts. He wants to
set us free from that pain. He wants us to give it to him
and trust God, to trust that God knows what he's doing,
even when it hurts. Even when we're scared or grieving,
God is still in control.

*If trust must be earned, hasn't God
unequivocally earned our trust with the bark
on the raw wounds, the thorns pressed into
the brow, your name on the cracked lips?*

ANN VOSKAMP

MY FATHER'S HOME

There is more than enough room in my Father's
home. If this were not so, would I have told you
that I am going to prepare a place for you?

JOHN 14:2

AS FOLLOWERS OF JESUS, we have so much to look forward to. One of these things is the Father's home, a home where there is more than enough room for all of us, a home Jesus is getting ready for us.

We don't know many details about this paradise that will be our eternal home, but doesn't the fact that your place will be prepared for you by Jesus himself tell you that you are in for a pretty spectacular eternity?

There in my Father's home, safe and at rest,
There in my Savior's love, perfectly blest;
Age after age to be nearer, my God, to Thee.

SARAH F. ADAMS

ONLY ONE WAY

*I am the way, the truth, and the life. No one
can come to the Father except through me.*

JOHN 14:6

THERE IS ONLY one way to God, and it's through Jesus.
But many people struggle with this truth, saying things
like "There are many paths to the truth" or "That's too
exclusive" or "Just figure out what works for you."

We cannot argue with these types of ideas. All we
can do is walk with Jesus, allow him to change us, and
hope that people see the difference in us because of the
joy and peace in our lives. Then they might say, "Maybe
there's something special to that Jesus after all." And we
can say, "Yes, there is."

*We come to God through Him—
or we don't come at all.*
ANNE GRAHAM LOTZ

THE GIFT

I will ask the Father, and he will give you
another Advocate, who will never leave you.

JOHN 14:16

IMAGINE HOW DEVASTATED the disciples were to lose
Jesus. First, they watched him die. Then they got him
back, only to watch him ascend to heaven.

But Jesus did not leave them—or you—alone. God
sent the Holy Spirit, the Advocate, a helper who *will never*
leave you. When you choose to follow Jesus, the Spirit
of God comes to live within you. How can we not live
inspired lives when we have God himself abiding in us?

Holy Spirit, Spirit of truth, you are the reward
of the saints, the comforter of souls, light in
the darkness, riches to the poor, treasure to
lovers, food for the hungry, comfort to those
who are wandering; to sum up, you are the
one in whom all treasures are contained.

MARY MAGDALENE DEI PAZZI

BELIEVE AND BEHAVE

Those who accept my commandments and obey them are the ones who love me. And because they love me, my Father will love them. And I will love them and reveal myself to each of them.

JOHN 14:21

WE DEMONSTRATE our love for Jesus by following his commands: love God completely, and love others. When we obey Jesus, he reveals himself to *each of us*.

Want to know Jesus intimately? Obey his commands. Want to see his hand in your life? Obey his commands. Want to be confident in his love for you? Obey his commands.

None of us can be perfect. That's why we need the Cross. But if we work to be obedient, we demonstrate our love to our Savior, and he rewards us by revealing himself to us.

There are two things to do about the Gospel—believe it and behave it.

SUSANNA WESLEY

 JUNE 4

GOD INSIDE YOU

*When the Father sends the Advocate as my
representative—that is, the Holy Spirit—he
will teach you everything and will remind
you of everything I have told you.*

JOHN 14:26

IF WE HAVE chosen to follow Jesus, we have the Holy
Spirit living inside us. Why do we tend to take the Holy
Spirit—the *Spirit of God*—for granted? Why do we spend
so much effort ignoring him or arguing with him?

The Holy Spirit has the power to change you, to
make you wiser, gentler, *better*. He can help you understand God's Word, lead you into contentment, and
awaken miraculous gifts within you. So let's give him
a chance. Let's find a quiet place and say, "Holy Spirit,
thank you for sticking with me."

*Allow the wild beauty of My Holy Spirit
to satiate your body, soul, and spirit right now.*

MARIE CHAPIAN

THE PEACE OF CHRIST

I am leaving you with a gift—peace of mind and heart. And the peace I give is a gift the world cannot give. So don't be troubled or afraid.

JOHN 14:27

NONBELIEVERS often notice the peace Christ gives us. *She just lost her job, and she doesn't even seem worried?* Or, *her child just died, and she's still praising God?* Or, *she has terminal cancer, and she's not angry or bitter?* It's hard for nonbelievers to understand what believers know: that bad things do happen, but a wise, loving God is in control and wins in the end.

The peace of Jesus is foreign to this world because it's not of this world. So seek it, reach for it, ask for it, and then enjoy it. And when people ask you how you have such peace, tell them!

Shalom is not the absence of trouble but the presence of Christ in the midst of our trouble.

SHEILA WALSH

NECESSARY PRUNING

*He cuts off every branch of mine that doesn't
produce fruit, and he prunes the branches that
do bear fruit so they will produce even more.*

JOHN 15:2

GOD WANTS US to produce "fruit"—godly attitudes, words, and works. But we're not born as full-grown fruit trees. Spiritual growth requires pruning, which often involves periods of suffering or discipline.

God prunes us because he loves us and wants us to mature in our faith. If our suffering leads someone to know the Lord, then isn't pruning worth it? If our discipline leads us to be better mothers or mentors, isn't it worth it?

*Just as the trees, if they have not stood before the
winter's storms cannot bear fruit, so it is with us;
this present age is a storm and it is only through
many trials and temptations that we can obtain
an inheritance in the kingdom of heaven.*

AMMA THEODORA

APART FROM ME

I am the vine; you are the branches. Those who remain in me, and I in them, will produce much fruit. For apart from me you can do nothing.

JOHN 15:5

JESUS TELLS US to remain in him—to gain nourishment from him, just as branches do from a vine. This means to stay close to him, to stay in the Word, to obey what he tells us, to not veer off into rabbit holes of sin, to keep the lines of communication open. So why do we so often think we can just do it ourselves? We won't get very far unless we let him have the driver's seat.

Without Me you can do nothing!
Live in Me, snuggled vitally united to Me,
for this is your sure path to
understanding who you are
and what you are called to do in this life.

MARIE CHAPIAN

GRANTED

*If you remain in me and my words
remain in you, you may ask for anything
you want, and it will be granted!*

JOHN 15:7

JESUS PROMISES THAT he will give us anything we want. But he doesn't promise to do it our way. We can ask him to provide for us, fix our problems, heal our wounds, save our loved ones, or deliver us from our strongholds, but then we need to let him do it his way, according to his schedule.

Jesus knows far more about what we want and need than we do. So if you pray for blueberry pie and you get raspberry, take a bite of the gifted pie. You might just think, *Wow! I do* like raspberry better!

*Jesus never gave a sermon on unanswered prayer
because, from his viewpoint, all prayers are answered.*

HOPE MACDONALD

TRUE JOY

I have told you these things so that you will be filled with my joy. Yes, your joy will overflow!

JOHN 15:11

JESUS SAYS THESE encouraging and powerful words right after teaching about love (see John 15:9-10). Women spend a lot of time and energy trying to find joy. We look for it in activities, in our jobs, in our families, and in our hobbies. Some of us try to find it in shopping, or food, or alcohol.

But there is only one source of the kind of joy that fills you and bubbles up to overflow onto others: the joy of Jesus' love. *That's* an eternal joy that is worth chasing after and that will automatically be shared with others.

A joyful heart is the normal result of a heart burning with love.... She gives most who gives with joy.

MOTHER TERESA

MAKE TIME FOR JESUS

*Anyone who belongs to God listens
gladly to the words of God.*

JOHN 8:47

THE WORD OF GOD is living and powerful, sharper than a sword (see Hebrews 4:12). So why do we sometimes struggle to get into it? Maybe because we all lead busy, distracted lives, and sometimes it's hard to just sit still and be with Jesus. It's hard to make the time to open the Bible and then focus on the words. It's hard to focus on the teaching when your kids are squirming in the pews or you've got to go to work after the service. Life is complicated.

But we can make it simpler. In fact, the more time we spend listening to the words of God, the less complicated life gets.

*The Bible is an ocean of instruction and wisdom.
Dip daily into the vast pool to discover its truths.*

ELIZABETH GEORGE

NO GREATER LOVE

*There is no greater love than to lay
down one's life for one's friends.*

JOHN 15:13

IF YOU HAVE CHILDREN, you would probably lay down your life for any of them in an instant. You can understand this "greater love" Jesus speaks of. But can you imagine doing it for the cranky woman at church? The homeless man who asks you for money? The murderer on death row?

Jesus *did* lay down his life for these people. And for you. And he would have done it for just one of us. If you were the only sinner on earth, he would still have gone willingly to the Cross. Because that's how much he loves you.

*He loved us to such an extent that He died for
us, irrespective of our condition or response.*

ANNE GRAHAM LOTZ

ALL TRUTH

*When the Spirit of truth comes, he
will guide you into all truth.*

JOHN 16:13

JESUS PROMISED his disciples—and us—that he would
send the Holy Spirit to guide us into all truth. Notice
Jesus didn't say "some truth" or "the basic truth"; he said
"all truth."

Every believer in Jesus has the Holy Spirit as a constant companion, helper, and guide. Because the Holy
Spirit will *guide* you into all truth, he will not *force* you
against your will. So you have to be willing to seek the
truth. And if you are willing, if you are earnestly seeking,
then the Holy Spirit will reveal it to you. He'll give you
as much truth as you need.

*Your own personal counselor, conscience,
and comforter fills your soul (mind, will,
and emotions) with perfect truth.*

JUNE HUNT

FROM SORROW TO JOY

It will be like a woman suffering the pains of labor. . . . Her anguish gives way to joy because she has brought a new baby into the world. So you have sorrow now, but I will see you again; then you will rejoice, and no one can rob you of that joy.

JOHN 16:21-22

JESUS USED THE PAIN of childbirth as a metaphor to help his disciples prepare for the pain of his departure: no mother looks back on the agony of labor and says it wasn't worth it. Jesus' disciples would someday understand their pain and rejoice when he returns.

Life is full of painful, difficult moments we're certain we won't survive. But one day, we will be able to look back on the sorrows of this life and realize they were worth it, because they led to eternal joy.

A thing that is lent may be taken away; a thing that is given is not taken away. Joy is given; sorrow is lent.

AMY CARMICHAEL

HE HAS ALREADY OVERCOME

Here on earth you will have many trials and sorrows.
But take heart, because I have overcome the world.

JOHN 16:33

WE LIVE IN A WORLD that is entirely contrary to Jesus' Kingdom, to his ways, to his teachings, to his heart. Our world is governed by Satan and his helpers, so it's no wonder we followers of Jesus don't exactly fit in.

When we find ourselves overwhelmed by the darkness in this world, we need to remember that its rule is short lived. Jesus has already won this war. We are just watching it play out. But we can be confident that we're on the winning side and it's just a matter of time.

The road ahead may include pain and suffering as part of God's plan, but thanks to Jesus's sacrifice, it ultimately leads to the glory of eternal life with him.

DIANNE NEAL MATTHEWS

THE WAY TO ETERNAL LIFE

This is the way to have eternal life—to know you, the only true God, and Jesus Christ, the one you sent to earth.

JOHN 17:3

ON THE NIGHT of his arrest, Jesus prayed to his Father in heaven, proclaiming aloud the path that leads to eternal life: know God, and know Jesus.

We can't earn eternal life. We can wear ourselves out going to church events, raising our children, and serving in the community, but none of that will get us to heaven. The only way to heaven is to know God. And the only way to know God is to know his Son.

Eternal life in the Kingdom of God is not a paycheck; it is a gift.

Thou hast made the end of this life the beginning to us of true life.

MACRINA THE YOUNGER

DOING GOD'S WORK

*I brought glory to you here on earth by
completing the work you gave me to do.*

JOHN 17:4

JESUS CAME TO EARTH with a specific purpose: to glorify God by doing God's will. What better goal could we aspire to? There is no higher calling. We can try to live like Jesus lived by doing God's will for our own lives, which will glorify God.

We find God's will through prayer, through being discipled by other believers, and by digging into his Word. And as we figure out God's will day by day, we can bring glory to him by obeying it. So, what is God telling you to do today?

*If you are able to finish God's work, it won't be
an accident. It'll be because you have focused
every minute of every day on God's purpose.*

ANNE GRAHAM LOTZ

YOU BELONG TO GOD

*All who are mine belong to you, and you have
given them to me, so they bring me glory.*

JOHN 17:10

JESUS PRAYED FOR his disciples—the people whom God
created and then gave to Jesus to teach and train. Though
they didn't know it, they had belonged to God since the
beginning, as we do as well.

We were born into this world only because God
willed it to be so. And though we've gone through periods of believing we were our own people, that we were
in charge of ourselves and our lives, this isn't exactly true.
We've belonged to God all along, and those of us who
acknowledge this will spend eternity in his presence.
Until then, we can live our lives in a way that brings
Jesus some of the glory he deserves.

The truest thing about you is the truth that you are his.

DEBBIE ALSDORF

PERFECT UNITY

*I have given them the glory you gave me, so they
may be one as we are one. I am in them and you
are in me. May they experience such perfect unity
that the world will know that you sent me.*

JOHN 17:22-23

UNITY IS CRUCIAL to the body of Christ, and Satan
knows this. So he works hard to distract Jesus' followers
from this knowledge. If we are spending our energy arguing about the sanctuary's curtains, about which books
go in the church library, and about whether the worship
team should sing hymns, we are so far down the rabbit
hole that we can't possibly accomplish anything for Jesus.

Imagine what would happen if we used a fraction of
that energy to actually seek God, talk to Jesus, and serve
others? We would change the world.

*I can have intimate fellowship with those
who come from a totally different background
than my own because we are one in Christ.*

NANCY DEMOSS WOLGEMUTH

HERE IS YOUR MOTHER

He said to this disciple, "Here is your mother." And from then on this disciple took her into his home.

JOHN 19:27

EVEN AS JESUS HUNG on the cross dying for humanity, he remembered one individual—his mother. Imagine her grief and horror as she stood there watching her son die such a painful, degrading death. But Jesus remembered her in that moment and made sure she would be taken care of after he died.

Mothers are important. We too must honor our mothers. And if you are a mother yourself, realize what a tremendous honor that is and try to enjoy it, even when it's most difficult. Your children will learn a lot about God's love by experiencing yours.

The loveliest masterpiece of the heart of God is the heart of a mother.

THÉRÈSE OF LISIEUX

MORE PROPHECY FULFILLED

I am thirsty.

JOHN 19:28

WHY DID JOHN preserve these words forever in Scripture? Jesus was human. He had human needs; he felt human pain and experienced human sensations.

But with these words, he also does something much more important. He fulfills a prophecy given in Psalm 69:21: "They give me poison [or gall] for food; they offer me sour wine for my thirst." Matthew 27:34 confirms that the soldiers gave Jesus wine mixed with gall as he hung on the cross, further showing the Jews that he was—and is—the Messiah they had been waiting for.

For those today who still doubt who Jesus is, these words whisper, "It's me. I'm the Savior."

> *And when*
> *I finally found*
> *You, Lord,*
> *Your bleeding hand was*
> *reaching for mine.*

SUSAN L. LENZKES

LAST WORDS

It is finished!

JOHN 19:30

THE LAST WORDS Jesus spoke from the cross were perhaps the most powerful words ever spoken: "It is finished." The battle was over. The war was won. The story would still play out through time, but at this point, the ending of the story was determined, and Jesus had won. He had defeated sin.

With these words, he declared that he had fulfilled every prophecy, met every need, redeemed every soul. With these words, he completed God's will and finished the plan God had put into place at the beginning. With these words, he crushed Satan's head. With these words, he spoke eternal life into your soul.

For there hangs God's Son in the balance,
And then through the darkness He cries—
It is finished!

GLORIA GAITHER

WHAT WE CLING TO

*"Don't cling to me," Jesus said, "for
I haven't yet ascended to the Father."*

JOHN 20:17

HOW WOULD YOU have reacted if you were Mary
Magdalene, seeing the risen Jesus for the first time? She
probably dropped her things, ran to him, and threw her
arms around him—at least until he said to her, "Don't
cling to me."

Jesus' words may seem a bit harsh, but he knew Mary
had an incomplete picture of God's plan for his Son.
Jesus, the risen Savior, would soon ascend to heaven and
send his Spirit to live within his followers. He was essentially telling Mary, "I can't stay here with you, because
I have much better things in store for you."

He has better things in store for you, too.

*Stop clinging so tightly to what you want. Don't
lose out on what God wants to give you.*

ANNE GRAHAM LOTZ

MARY THE MESSENGER

Go find my brothers and tell them,
"I am ascending to my Father and your
Father, to my God and your God."

JOHN 20:17

GOD CHOSE WOMEN to discover the empty tomb. Mary Magdalene was one of the first to touch the resurrected Jesus, who gave her the important job of delivering the news of his miracle to his other disciples. In a similar way, he chose the Samaritan woman at the well to deliver the news of the Messiah's arrival to her village (see John 4:1-42).

This is a God who loves and values women. This is a Savior who came to rescue men and women alike, who entrusts both men and women with important Kingdom tasks.

God placed himself in a woman's care when he
came to earth, then entrusted a woman to announce
his resurrection when he came back to life.

LIZ CURTIS HIGGS

DOUBTING THOMAS

Put your finger here, and look at my hands.
Put your hand into the wound in my side.
Don't be faithless any longer. Believe!

JOHN 20:27

POOR THOMAS. Though he followed Jesus around for years, he's best remembered for the time he doubted him.

Notice, however, that Thomas's doubts did not keep him away from Jesus. Thomas was not stubborn about his doubts, nor did he use them as a reason to run away. Also notice that Jesus didn't scold Thomas. Instead, he just patiently said, "Here I am. It's really me."

Doubts are natural. But we need to be honest and up front with Jesus when we have these doubts. He already knows our hearts. We might as well say, "Jesus, I'm doubting this right now. Please increase my faith."

Faith does not eliminate questions. But
faith knows where to take them.

ELISABETH ELLIOT

LIMITLESS

A third time [Jesus] asked him, "Simon son of John, do you love me?"

JOHN 21:17

BEFORE JESUS' CRUCIFIXION, Simon Peter had shamefully denied knowing Jesus (see, for example, John 18). Later Jesus asked him three times, "Do you love me?"—one for each of the times Peter had denied him. In this way, Jesus showed Peter that he was completely forgiven of his denial.

Sometimes we think we've made the same bad decision too many times to recover from it. But this is a lie. When we are truly repentant, Jesus forgives—even if we deny him three times.

The grace of Jesus Christ is limitless.

Grace isn't about having a second chance; grace is having so many chances that you could use them through all eternity and never come up empty. It's when you finally realize that the other shoe isn't going to drop, ever.

SHAUNA NIEQUIST

GIVING

It is more blessed to give than to receive.

ACTS 20:35

GENEROSITY MIGHT not feel like a natural inclination, but it should be. We are created in God's image, and God is the greatest gift giver of all. Just think of all he has provided for you—starting with his Son, Jesus.

So what if we're not very good at giving? These words from Jesus might inspire us to keep trying until we get better at it. According to Jesus, the giver is blessed. Want to be blessed? Give. And then give some more. It won't take long for you to prove Jesus right.

So many times in life we try to protect what we value, but we are doubly blessed when we give it away. Have you given away your love today? Have you shared your faith? If not, what are you waiting for?

TRICIA GOYER

THE LOVELESS CHURCH

*I have this complaint against you. You don't
love me or each other as you did at first!*

REVELATION 2:4

THE CHURCH IN EPHESUS had forgotten about love! Jesus
had to remind them to come back to it. In 1 Corinthians
13:1-3, the apostle Paul writes, "If I could speak all the
languages of earth . . . but didn't love others, I would only
be a noisy gong or a clanging cymbal. If I had the gift of
prophecy . . . but didn't love others, I would be nothing.
If I gave everything I have to the poor . . . but if I didn't
love others, I would have gained nothing."

We can be the biggest, fastest, smartest, prettiest
Christians in town, but if we are operating without love,
we're doing it all in vain.

*Jesus wants our love for Him before
He wants our work for Him.*

ANNE GRAHAM LOTZ

KNOCKING AT THE DOOR

*Look! I stand at the door and knock. If you hear
my voice and open the door, I will come in, and
we will share a meal together as friends.*

REVELATION 3:20

JESUS SPOKE THESE words to the church in Laodicea, also
called the Lukewarm Church (see Revelation 3:16). This
letter wasn't intended for those on fire for Christ but for
those with complacent faith.

Even still, Jesus let them (and us) know that he is still
knocking. He doesn't give up. All we have to do is open
the door, and he will come in and have a meal with us.
He's not going to bust down the door, though. He's just
going to knock. The rest is up to us.

*Open to Me, look on Me eye to eye,
That I may wring thy heart and make it whole.*

CHRISTINA ROSSETTI

MORNING STAR

I, Jesus, have sent my angel to give you this message for the churches. I am both the source of David and the heir to his throne. I am the bright morning star.

REVELATION 22:16

WHEN JESUS ROSE from the dead, he ushered in a new day, a new way of being for anyone who chooses it. All who look up at him will gain a new understanding of life. The first time we see the morning star for what he is, our lives change.

And they continue to change with each earthly morning we face. Each day is a new day, a clean slate that gives us a chance to live as new creations, to walk in Jesus' freedom, light, and love.

Morning Star, I trust You with tomorrow
As You guide me through the dark
With the light of Your plan.

REBECCA J. PECK

SOON

Yes, I am coming soon!
REVELATION 22:20

EVERYTHING WE EXPERIENCE in this lifetime—all our joys and pains—exist within the mighty shadow of this promise. These words are the last recorded words of Jesus in the Bible, but they say it all.

We live here on earth, in this frail human form, knowing that Jesus will come back to earth and bring his story to completion. And we know that we will be on the winning side, because we belong to him, the one who will reign forever from his heavenly throne. We will be right there with him. Forever.

*Mine eyes have seen the glory of
the coming of the Lord:
He is trampling out the vintage where
the grapes of wrath are stored;
He hath loosed the fateful lightning
of His terrible swift sword:
His truth is marching on.*

JULIA WARD HOWE

INTEGRITY

Just say a simple, "Yes, I will," or "No, I won't."
Anything beyond this is from the evil one.

MATTHEW 5:37

IF YOU ARE A WOMAN who keeps it simple and keeps her word, you are a rarity. If you say what you mean and mean what you say, you are making waves in this world. If you are consistently honest, people take notice, and they begin to trust you. After a while, you don't have to prove yourself anymore. People will consider you and your word as good as gold.

If you are a woman with integrity, you are a treasure. People will depend on you and want you in their lives.

A godly woman is beyond average because she
keeps her word. She honors her vows. She exhibits
great faith. She overcomes great obstacles. And she
affects her family, her community, even the world.

ELIZABETH GEORGE

NO OFFENSE

Forgive us our sins,
as we have forgiven those who sin against us.

MATTHEW 6:12

SOME PEOPLE ACT as if the state of being offended is virtuous. If we walk around supremely offended, then we must be righteous, right? Wrong. Holding on to the harmful things people say and do against us alienates us from our Savior. If we have placed our trust in Jesus, then we have experienced forgiveness and received *his* righteousness. How can we hold on to bitterness when he has given his life to clear our offenses against him?

When we forgive "those who sin against us," we love like Jesus loves. It sets us free for much bigger and better things.

Don't forget what people intend to use for harm,
God can use for His greater good. Let offenses
slide today, and watch how God works!

ALISA HOPE WAGNER

EVIL THOUGHTS

*Jesus knew what they were thinking, so
he asked them, "Why do you have such
evil thoughts in your hearts?"*

MATTHEW 9:4

WE TALK ABOUT how evil the world is, and that is true, but do we pay much attention to how much of that evil resides in our own hearts? We can't conquer the evil of this world, but we can, with God's help, kick the evil out of ourselves.

Have we repented of all we've done and thought so we can start with a clean slate right now? Have we forgiven anyone who has ever wronged us? Have we forgiven ourselves for our mistakes and bad decisions? And when a new evil thought or feeling does appear, do we kick it out immediately?

*We rant and rave against God for the evil we have to
endure but hardly blink at the evil in our own hearts.*

JONI EARECKSON TADA

FOCUS ON TODAY

Don't worry about tomorrow, for tomorrow will bring its own worries. Today's trouble is enough for today.

MATTHEW 6:34

BY TELLING US not to worry about tomorrow, Jesus freed us up to live with peace, contentment, and joy today.

We cannot enjoy today and all its blessings, both big and small, if we are worrying about what will happen tomorrow. So don't do it! Don't fall into this trap! Live today just for today. Enjoy every moment God gives you—the smile of a loved one, the sound of birdsong, the sunshine on your skin, the taste of good food.

Today is a gift. Live it well. Use it to honor God. Enjoy *this* day. Deal with tomorrow tomorrow.

Worry does not empty tomorrow of its sorrow; it empties today of its strength.

CORRIE TEN BOOM

BECAUSE OF YOUR FAITH

Because of your faith, it will happen.
MATTHEW 9:29

TWO BLIND MEN believed that Jesus could heal them, and it happened (see Matthew 9:27-29).

But what if it hadn't happened? Would they have still believed? When we ask Jesus to heal cancer, knowing that he certainly can, sometimes he does. And we celebrate and give him all the praise. But sometimes he doesn't. And we still need to celebrate and give him all the praise—because he is God, and he knows what he's doing.

None of us want to suffer. We don't want our loved ones to suffer. But the best thing we can do for ourselves is to surrender to God. The best thing we can do for our loved ones is to place them in Jesus' loving hands.

To believe is to give God the right to answer our prayer in the way he sees best.
HOPE MACDONALD

SPIRIT, SPEAK

Don't worry about how to respond or what to say.
God will give you the right words at the right time.
For it is not you who will be speaking—it will be
the Spirit of your Father speaking through you.

MATTHEW 10:19-20

WHAT GREAT NEWS! So many of us are uncomfortable with speaking in front of a crowd. What would happen if we had to do it in defense of our faith? It would be all right!

Jesus promised that when you struggle to clearly articulate what you believe about him, the Holy Spirit will give you the words. It won't be you but the Spirit of God who will be speaking through you.

I pray that the Holy Spirit puts His Words
in my mouth, His movement in my heart
and His direction in my path.

ALISA HOPE WAGNER

ACQUITTAL, PLEASE!

*I tell you this, you must give an account on judgment
day for every idle word you speak. The words
you say will either acquit you or condemn you.*

MATTHEW 12:36-37

YIKES! Every single word? You mean that small, juicy,
unverified tidbit we shared at Bible study? Or the time we
overshared about our marital frustrations? Or the white
lies? Or the time we snapped at our kids? Or the time we
snapped at someone else's kids?

What if we took every word as seriously as Jesus suggested? What if we thought before we spoke? What if we
consulted the Holy Spirit before we spoke? Wouldn't it
be great if our words acquitted us instead of condemning
us when we stand before Jesus?

*Beauty should be the goal for all of
your communication. . . . Learn to
speak with godly wisdom.*

ELIZABETH GEORGE

GOOD SOIL

The seed that fell on good soil represents those
who truly hear and understand God's word
and produce a harvest of thirty, sixty, or even a
hundred times as much as had been planted!

MATTHEW 13:23

YOU ARE GOOD SOIL. When the seed of the gospel landed on you, it sprouted into something beautiful and mighty. And before long, you were producing seeds of your own.

Are you afraid to cast those seeds around? Don't be! It is sad that some of them won't find good soil to land in. But some of them will. And those seeds will also sprout and result in more seeds.

There is more good soil out there. There are future sisters waiting.

Sharing the truth about Jesus—the Gospel—
is . . . like breaking open a pod and setting
the seeds loose with a puff of our breath.

CYNTHIA RUCHTI

NOT EVEN ONE

*In the same way, it is not my heavenly Father's will
that even one of these little ones should perish.*

MATTHEW 18:14

GOD WANTS TO SAVE every single one of us: even the
stubborn, the angry, the arrogant. Every single person
you lay eyes on this week is loved by God, and he wants
them to be his.

But God did not create a robot species. Robots cannot love. He created us, humans, who can choose to love
or choose not to. God does not force himself on anyone.
He simply issues an invitation. It is up to the individuals he created to accept it. And when one does accept
it, there is a celebration in heaven as God reclaims that
child as his own.

*There is nothing that moves a loving
father's soul quite like his child's cry.*

JONI EARECKSON TADA

GOD KNOWS THE DETAILS

*If God cares so wonderfully for flowers that
are here today and thrown into the fire
tomorrow, he will certainly care for you.*

LUKE 12:28

JESUS IS SAYING in this verse that God is a God of details.
Sometimes it is tempting to think he's too busy running
the universe to take notice of our small problems, emotions, or struggles. But that is a lie.

There is no limit to God's power, so he has plenty of
it left to be aware of and involved in your life. He knows
how many hairs are on your head. He knows every cor-
ner of your heart. He knows you better than you know
yourself. He created you.

*Flowers feed our soul in a different way. They
remind us of a God who creates beautiful
things and takes notice of the tiniest detail.*

TRICIA GOYER

OUT OF THE MOUTHS OF BABES

*Haven't you ever read the Scriptures?
For they say, "You have taught children
and infants to give you praise."*

MATTHEW 21:16

THE CHILDREN WERE shouting praises to Jesus, which irritated the leading priests and teachers of the law (see Matthew 21:15). "Do you hear what these kids are saying?" they asked. "I sure do," Jesus said, and then he quoted King David (see Psalm 8:2).

If you've spent any time with children, you've probably noticed how readily their lips praise Jesus. It seems to come so naturally to them, as if they were born with this innate knowledge of his glory. Young children are often the boldest in praise and the bravest in witnessing. Sometimes we need to act more like children.

*The hope that danced from the children's mouths
in praise was unmistakable and unmissable.*

ERIN KEELEY MARSHALL

DON'T LET YOUR LOVE GROW COLD

*Sin will be rampant everywhere, and the
love of many will grow cold. But the one
who endures to the end will be saved.*

MATTHEW 24:12-13

JESUS SPOKE OF a future time when everywhere we look
we would see depravity, when even believers would not
seem to be walking in love. Sound familiar?

Sin may be rampant, but Jesus doesn't want us to stop
loving. We need to keep on loving, so that those who are
lost might see that love and decide they want to experience
it for themselves, straight from the source. Jesus wants us
to persevere in loving others—to love boldly, bravely, indis-
criminately; to love even when it's difficult; to love people
who don't even seem to want our love or his.

*Perseverance and staying? These are active. Staying
is a willful choice. Perseverance results in triumph.*

ELIZABETH GEORGE

KEEP WATCH AND PRAY

*Keep watch and pray, so that you will
not give in to temptation. For the spirit
is willing, but the body is weak!*

MATTHEW 26:41

THE GOOD NEWS: our spirits are willing to obey God.
The bad news: our bodies are weak. We want to change,
we want to live for Jesus, but temptation doesn't leave
us alone.

Sometimes we let our guard down. Sometimes we fall
for traps, and we sin. But that's not the end of the story
for us. Jesus wants to pick us right back up and stand
us up straight. And when he does, we need to vigilantly
"keep watch and pray."

*We can't afford to be complacent about God's glory.
The fact is that putting your Christian life on
autopilot is the same thing as "walking in the flesh."*

JONI EARECKSON TADA

NEW WINE

No one puts new wine into old wineskins.
For the wine would burst the wineskins,
and the wine and the skins would both be
lost. New wine calls for new wineskins.

MARK 2:22

JESUS EXPLAINED to his critics that he was ushering in a new way of doing things. He was the "new wine," and he couldn't be poured into "old wineskins." He was creating a new covenant, which wouldn't fit in with their way of thinking: strict adherence to a lifeless law.

Thank God for the new way! Under the old system, we could never be good enough. Despite how much the Pharisees revered it, the law was never supposed to be the be-all and end-all—its purpose was to show us our need for Jesus. Mission accomplished!

Legalism and focus on my own efforts
don't fit with the new wine of grace.
SHARON HINCK

YOU WHO ARE POOR

God blesses you who are poor,
for the Kingdom of God is yours.

LUKE 6:20

IN OUR WORLD, there is no shortage of those who go without. But Jesus has good news for people in need. He identifies with the poor. He came into this world as one of them, grew up as one of them, served them during his earthly ministry, died for them, and rose from the dead for them. For those who believe, he gifts them with eternal life and brings them into the Kingdom of God.

Those of us who have enough may be tempted to ignore, belittle, or blame those who do not have enough. What would Jesus say to that?

Remember, Christ willed to be born poor, and He chose disciples who were living, for the most part, in poverty. Christ made Himself a servant of poor people.

JONI EARECKSON TADA

POURED INTO YOUR LAP

*Give, and you will receive. Your gift will return
to you in full—pressed down, shaken together
to make room for more, running over, and
poured into your lap. The amount you give
will determine the amount you get back.*

LUKE 6:38

WHILE WE SHOULDN'T selfishly do something just so that
we can get something in return, today's verse contains a
sweet promise straight from Jesus' lips. We will be blessed
according to how we bless others. This may not always
mean material blessings, but certainly it means the spiritual
ones, which are the ones that really matter, the ones
we take with us.

Can you think of something you could do for someone
right now? Now imagine that coming back to you, only
multiplied, overflowing, and even more full of blessing.

*We can give richly, serve sacrificially, and love
unconditionally . . . as we follow Jesus' example.*

ELIZABETH GEORGE

NO COMPROMISE

Anyone who isn't with me opposes me,
and anyone who isn't working with me
is actually working against me.

LUKE 11:23

PART OF WORKING with Jesus is sharing the gospel without compromise. We are sometimes tempted to compromise our faith because we want people to see us as welcoming, forgiving, and nonjudgmental. But these attributes do not require compromise, because the gospel *is* welcoming, forgiving, and nonjudgmental. Jesus doesn't need us to tweak his message to make it more palatable. We don't have to water down the gospel or jazz it up. It's perfect just the way it is.

We need to make sure that no matter what, we are working on Jesus' side, because if we're not working for him, we're working against him—and that's not where we want to be.

When it comes to Jesus, there is no middle ground.
DIANNE NEAL MATTHEWS

CLUTTER

[Jesus] told them a story: "A rich man ... said,
'I know! I'll tear down my barns and build
bigger ones. Then I'll have room enough to
store all my wheat and other goods.'"

LUKE 12:16, 18

WE CAN ALL FALL prey to hoarding. Many of us like to keep trinkets, memorabilia, keepsakes: our grandmother's cracked teacup, a first date concert ticket, our daughter's soccer trophy. We are afraid to get rid of things we "might need": books, picture frames, pants that are a little too snug. Some things are just "too good" to pitch: broken crayons, single earrings.

Do we add on, build a garage, rent a storage unit? Is saving all this stuff consuming our lives and keeping us from loving others and sharing the gospel with them?

If we clear out the clutter, what blessings might we make room for?

Jesus is teaching us something simple about
wisdom, the older we grow: keep it simple.

REBECCA BARLOW JORDAN

THE NARROW DOOR

Work hard to enter the narrow door to God's Kingdom, for many will try to enter but will fail.

LUKE 13:24

JESUS OPENS HIS ARMS to anyone, right? So why is it a narrow door? And why do we have to work hard to enter it? Don't we just have to walk through it?

Jesus knew that people would struggle with surrendering their lives to him. He knew that people would have to swallow their pride and admit their need for a Savior. People would have to admit that they couldn't save themselves. This confession is the narrow door of the Kingdom, one that is difficult to pass through. Let's patiently keep telling others how beautiful life is on the other side.

The gate is narrow but not the life. The gate opens out into largeness of life.

ELISABETH ELLIOT

TO SIT OR TO SERVE

*Who is more important, the one who sits
at the table or the one who serves? The one
who sits at the table, of course. But not here!
For I am among you as one who serves.*

LUKE 22:27

WHETHER OR NOT we're wives and moms, we women often find ourselves serving others. And this is a good thing, but it can get exhausting.

Jesus knows what it means to serve. This should encourage us in our difficult moments of service—like when we organize a meal and someone snaps at us about the lack of dietary options, or when we're coaching that peewee softball game and a parent hollers at us.

Jesus sees your heart as you serve others. He is pleased with your efforts. He has been there.

*No service, no matter how insignificant we may
consider it, goes unnoticed or unappreciated by God.*

KATHERINE BRAZELTON

FROM RAGS TO RIGHTEOUSNESS

God sent his Son into the world not to judge the world, but to save the world through him.

JOHN 3:17

HAVE YOU EVER looked back on a difficult situation and realized, *That turned out all right*? Thank you, Jesus! Have you ever struggled to overcome some sin and then helped someone else do the same? Thank you, Jesus! Have you ever stopped trying to control someone you love and then watched God take hold of them in a mighty way? Thank you, Jesus!

Jesus came to this earth to cover our bad decisions with his grace. Now, God uses all those things for his purpose and for our own good. Thank you, Jesus!

It is God's deepest desire to bless mankind. . . . As a result, whenever it becomes necessary for God's righteousness to judge for disobedience, His love also provides a way to turn that punishment into blessing.

VIRGINIA RUTH FUGATE

OBEDIENCE

I know all the things you do, and I have
opened a door for you that no one can
close. You have little strength, yet you
obeyed my word and did not deny me.

REVELATION 3:8

JESUS KNOWS WE have weaknesses. He knows we won't
be perfect. He just asks us to obey him, to not deny him,
even when we have little strength.

Obedience is so crucial to having a close walk with
Jesus. And the rewards are great. Jesus sees our hearts
and everything we do, and when we obey even in our
weakness, he opens doors for us to serve him in even
greater ways.

Ask Jesus to help you fully understand
the joys of obedience.

LYSA TERKEURST

THOSE CLOSEST

*This is my commandment: Love each other
in the same way I have loved you.*

JOHN 15:12

JESUS TALKS a lot about loving one another. Sometimes
we women automatically jump to loving those whom *we*
think need love the most. We join the missions team. We
sponsor a child in India. We volunteer at the inner-city
soup kitchen. We love on people we don't know.

Sometimes we forget that we also need to love those
closest to us. Jesus' commandment does not exclude those
in our homes, on our streets, in our churches. It doesn't
exclude our husbands or boyfriends, our neighbors, our
children and grandchildren, our parents and siblings, or
our coworkers and bosses. Sometimes the best opportunities to obey Jesus' command are within arm's reach.

*Love begins by taking care of the
closest ones—the ones at home.*

MOTHER TERESA

EVEN GREATER WORKS

*I tell you the truth, anyone who believes in me will
do the same works I have done, and even greater
works, because I am going to be with the Father.*

JOHN 14:12

TALK ABOUT DROPPING a bombshell! Jesus said those who
believe in him will do "the same works" and "even greater
works" than he did. How is that possible?

When Jesus was on earth, he was limited to just one
body. Today there are millions of people who have God's
Spirit within them. If we were all seeking God, living for
Jesus, and loving others, just think of what we could do!

Is this how we are living? Or are we just plodding
along, struggling to survive the day? How much more
could we accomplish if we really took these words of
Jesus to heart?

*When we set our sights high, we
get a better look at Him.*

DIANNE NEAL MATTHEWS

SUFFICIENT GRACE

My grace is all you need.

2 CORINTHIANS 12:9

THE APOSTLE PAUL was struggling with something he called a thorn in his flesh (see 2 Corinthians 12:7). Three times he asked the Lord to take away this burden. But Jesus said, "My grace is all you need."

Grace. Undeserved favor. Unconditional love. Jesus gives us enough of it to get us through the thorn, through the day, and through eternity.

Like Paul, we will face difficult things. You're probably facing something difficult right now. But Jesus' grace is enough to get you through it. Lean on Jesus. Push into him. Seek him with all your heart. Call out to him. He is there for you, ready to pour out his grace on your life.

Victory is ours in Christ. His grace is sufficient.
Know this truth and it will set you free.

JONI EARECKSON TADA

WHEN WE ARE WEAK, WE ARE STRONG

My power works best in weakness.

2 CORINTHIANS 12:9

WHEN EVERYTHING is going well and we think we are strong, we like to dance around singing, "I can do it!"

But then we fall. And suddenly, we are aware of our need for Jesus. Suddenly, we are aware of our own weakness. Suddenly, we are no longer puffed up with the pride that gets between us and our real source of power.

When we are weak, we are forced to lean on Jesus for help. When we lean on him the most, we get his power. So when we are at our weakest, we are really at our strongest.

We like to look at our weakness, but Jesus looks at His own strength. We focus on our limits, but Jesus knows He's limitless. Because we can't achieve our dreams on our own, we get to see Jesus-at-work in us.

TRICIA GOYER

THE TREE OF LIFE

To everyone who is victorious I will give fruit
from the tree of life in the paradise of God.

REVELATION 2:7

HOW CAN WE be victorious? Well, we can't be. Not without some help. But we have help, don't we? The one who made the promise in today's verse—Jesus—has swooped in and saved the day. If we accept his gift, if we enter into his victory, then we can be victorious too.

The tree of life, the tree that sustains eternal life, stood in the center of the Garden of Eden. Now it stands in paradise, where thanks to Jesus' gift, you will spend eternity. Jesus defeated death so that you could eat of the tree of life. It doesn't get much more victorious than that.

You tasted death for me . . .
You gave Yourself so freely
To finally help us find the tree of life.

LISA PROKOPOWITZ

WHAT YOU BELIEVED
AT FIRST

*Go back to what you heard and believed at
first; hold to it firmly. Repent and turn to me
again. If you don't wake up, I will come to
you suddenly, as unexpected as a thief.*

REVELATION 3:3

SOME OF US CAME to Jesus long ago. Some of us even
came as children. Once you've been with Jesus for a
while, it can become easy to take him for granted. In
today's verse he's warning us not to.

Sometimes it's necessary to get back to basics, to
remember what Jesus did to save us and what he has saved
us from. Sometimes we need to repent of the things that
we've let creep in between our Savior and us. Sometimes
it's necessary to say, again, "Here is my life. Do with it
what you will."

Surrender is the only path to supernatural living.
ALISA HOPE WAGNER

NEVER ERASED

*All who are victorious will be clothed in
white. I will never erase their names from the
Book of Life, but I will announce before my
Father and his angels that they are mine.*

REVELATION 3:5

IMAGINE ENTERING a new place on your Savior's arm.
You don't quite recognize it, yet it feels familiar to you.
You're dressed all in white, like a pure bride, because his
blood has washed away your filth. And as you enter, a
gentle but firm voice introduces you to God and the
angels, saying, "She is mine."

As you look around, you can scarcely believe your
eyes. Not only is everything you see beyond whatever
you'd imagined, but you know this, your new home, is
for good. Permanent. Your name will never be erased.
Welcome to paradise.

*With God's help, your trial today is leading
to your wholeness tomorrow.*

ELIZABETH GEORGE

THE BEGINNING AND THE END

I am the Alpha and the Omega, the First and the Last, the Beginning and the End.

REVELATION 22:13

ALPHA AND *OMEGA* are the first and last letters of the Greek alphabet. It's so hard for us to understand the beginning and the end of something eternal. It's hard for us to understand God's sense of time, when all we know is our own.

Trying to understand God's ways can make us feel like children in a calculus class. Thank Jesus that we don't have to understand. All we need to do is trust that Jesus *is* the beginning and the end. And he's everything in the middle. He's everything, period.

He is the One Who started it all, and He is the One Who will bring it to a conclusion. He is what life is all about.

REBECCA BARLOW JORDAN

PRAY LIKE THIS

Pray like this: Our Father in heaven,
may your name be kept holy.

JESUS TAUGHT HIS followers how to pray, and he began his prayer with praise. How often do we begin our prayer with a laundry list of our needs, wants, or demands? How much more would our prayers please God if we began with simple praise? How about a laundry list of the amazing things he's already done for us?

It's also worth noting that Jesus starts out his exemplary prayer with the words "Our Father." This suggests we should be praying together—praying and praising with our brothers and sisters, young and old.

Thy name be hallowed
morning, noon and night,
in the quiet pulse of darkness,
in the harpstrings of the light.

KAY SMITH

CHOICES

Don't let us yield to temptation,
but rescue us from the evil one.

MATTHEW 6:13

WOULDN'T IT BE GREAT IF, once we began to follow Jesus, we never had to deal with temptation again? But that isn't the way it works.

Sometimes it seems like the more closely we follow Jesus, the more we are aware of what offends him, and the more temptations we face. We may face a thousand temptations per day. We know we will face them, and we don't want to face them alone, so we ask God to protect us, to rescue us. We thank Jesus for the victory of the Cross, and then we ask the Holy Spirit to help us walk within that victory. We ask him to help us make choices that will honor Jesus.

I live life one choice at a time.
REBECCA MULVANEY

A HOUSE THAT WILL STAND

*Anyone who listens to my teaching and follows it is
wise, like a person who builds a house on solid rock.*

MATTHEW 7:24

JESUS HAS TO BE the foundation of our faith. We have to
start with him as our Savior and then build from there.
If we try to build on something else—our parents' values,
our traditions, our talents, our careers, our wealth, even
our families—our houses will come crashing down.

Jesus is our solid rock. When we build our lives
on him and his words, nothing can tear down our
salvation—not grief, not pain, not illness, not violence,
not persecution, not even death. When we build on Jesus,
we are building a house that will carry us into eternity.

*For the winds of the dawn say, "Follow, follow
Jesus Bar-Joseph, the carpenter's son."*

MARJORIE L. C. PICKTHALL

THE VERY HAIRS ON YOUR HEAD

The very hairs on your head are all numbered.
MATTHEW 10:30

PEOPLE OFTEN QUOTE this verse because it's such a crazy thing to imagine. Just how many hairs *are* on our heads? As crazy as it is to try to count them, we really do serve a God who knows the exact amount. We can't lose a hair or grow a new one without him knowing. He knows when each one turns gray (and whether we promptly yank it out or dye it).

How can we doubt a God like this? He knows what's going on in our relationships, in our families, in our jobs, in our hearts. He knows and he cares. So next time you're feeling alone, run your fingers through your hair!

He who cares for the sparrows, and numbers the hairs of our head, cannot possibly fail us.
HANNAH WHITALL SMITH

SHINE LIKE THE SUN

*The righteous will shine like the sun in
their Father's Kingdom. Anyone with ears
to hear should listen and understand!*

MATTHEW 13:43

ONE DAY, JESUS will send his angels to remove from our midst everything that causes sin. They will also remove the sinners, those who refuse to accept Jesus' gift of redemption. However, those of us who have chosen Jesus have a bright future ahead. We will "shine like the sun"!

Until then, there are days when we won't feel very bright. Our lives won't seem shiny. They may even seem dull or dark. But that doesn't change our future. No matter what happens today, Jesus has given us the security of an eternity with him. We can count on it.

*Maintaining an eternal perspective is key
to responding to the challenges we face
now. Heaven is our permanent home,
and it is truly going to be glorious!*

CYNTHIA HEALD

MOVING MOUNTAINS

You don't have enough faith. . . . I tell you
the truth, if you had faith even as small as a
mustard seed, you could say to this mountain,
"Move from here to there," and it would
move. Nothing would be impossible.

MATTHEW 17:20

CAN YOU IMAGINE bossing a mountain around? And yet Jesus said that's what faith can do. Faith in Jesus heals broken hearts. It heals broken marriages. Faith in Jesus changes lives. It saves lives. Faith in Jesus heals people from illness, from anger, from bitterness, from hopelessness. Faith in Jesus brings dead souls to life.

We will face mountains in this lifetime. You may even be facing one right now. You don't have to submit to it. A little faith goes a long way.

Faith is a supernatural confidence
that God's promises are true.

LINDA PAGE

ON HIS BEHALF

Anyone who welcomes a little child like
this on my behalf is welcoming me.

MATTHEW 18:5

WHAT GREAT NEWS for those of us involved in the lives of children! Jesus loves children. They are beloved by him. They are crucial to his Kingdom. They are not just adults in formation—they are already precious souls in his sight. He calls them to himself, and he teaches them, protects them, and uses them to accomplish his beautiful purpose on earth.

Not all of us are called to minister to children. But all of us can be praying for the children we know, asking Jesus to draw them close and keep them there.

He wanted children by His side,
stretched out His arms, stood,
beckoned you,
called Come to me
and died
in your place
so that you could.

LUCI SHAW

THE VINEYARD WORKERS

I haven't been unfair! Didn't you agree to work all day for the usual wage? Take your money and go. I wanted to pay this last worker the same as you. Is it against the law for me to do what I want with my money? Should you be jealous because I am kind to others?

MATTHEW 20:13-15

IN THE PARABLE of the vineyard workers, Jesus gently warned us against looking down our noses at those who've just found him. Instead of arrogantly comparing our level of spirituality to theirs, we need to welcome these brothers and sisters and surround them in the love of Jesus where they can grow and flourish. Let's rejoice that we serve a generous God who offers salvation even to those who come at the last minute.

Shall I find comfort, travel-sore and weak?
Of labour you shall find the sum.
Will there be beds for me and all who seek?
Yea, beds for all who come.

CHRISTINA ROSSETTI

JESUS DESIRES COMPANIONSHIP

My soul is crushed with grief to the point of death. Stay here and keep watch with me.

MATTHEW 26:38

JESUS KNEW HE was going to die. He knew it was God's will. He knew it was necessary for our salvation, and he loved us enough to go through with it. But still, he was human enough to dread it. He was fully God, but he was also fully a man, a man experiencing a crushing grief. And he wanted his friends. He asked them to stay there with him and keep him company.

Jesus' love for us is not an abstract idea. It is a reality. And because he loves us, he wants us to spend time with him.

We tend to view our times with the Lord strictly for our benefit. How our perspective changes when we realize that the Lord Himself longs for our companionship.

CYNTHIA HEALD

BLOW US AWAY

*Go out where it is deeper, and let down
your nets to catch some fish.*

LUKE 5:4

IMAGINE! A complete stranger shows up out of nowhere and tells you how to do your job. How would you respond? Peter, James, and John must have recognized something special about Jesus, because they did what he said. Though they knew plenty about fishing, they still took his fishing advice. And the results blew them away. In fact, the results impressed them so much, they promptly dropped their lives and followed Jesus (see Luke 5:5-11).

So often we think we know what we are doing. But if we would simply follow Jesus' instructions, the results would blow us away too.

*Look to the Master, follow His directions and
then put forth the effort to pull in the net. Your
net will be filled with gladness and joy.*

AMY BOLDING

YOU WHO WEEP NOW

God blesses you who weep now,
for in due time you will laugh.

LUKE 6:21

THIS LIFE IS FULL of such heartbreak. Who knows the grief of a lonely widow or a parent who loses a child? Who knows the grief from abandonment or a broken marriage? Who knows the grief brought by chronic pain or terminal illness?

Jesus. That's who. He knows all our pain, and he bears it with us. You never weep alone, my friend. And those of us who weep a lot in this lifetime have lots more laughter in store. One day we will all be laughing together in paradise.

The will of God is never exactly what you expect
it to be. It may seem to be much worse, but in the
end it's going to be a lot better and a lot bigger.

ELISABETH ELLIOT

STAND

I tell you the truth, everyone who acknowledges
me publicly here on earth, the Son of Man will also
acknowledge in the presence of God's angels.

LUKE 12:8

SOMETIMES IT IS DIFFICULT to take a stand for Jesus. You might be ridiculed by your peers. You might be shunned by your family. You might be passed over for the promotion. You might even be fired. You might lose friends.

But you will be rewarded. Jesus will boldly speak the names of those who take a stand for him in front of his Father and the angels. Nothing in this life can compete with that.

> *Beneath the cross of Jesus*
> *I gladly take my stand,*
> *the shadow of a mighty rock*
> *within a weary land;*
> *a home within the wilderness,*
> *a rest upon the way,*
> *from the burning of the noontide heat,*
> *and the burden of the day.*

ELIZABETH C. CLEPHANE

BEFORE IT'S TOO LATE

*When the master of the house has locked the
door, it will be too late. You will stand outside
knocking and pleading, "Lord, open the door
for us!" But he will reply, "I don't know you."*

LUKE 13:25

WE KNOW THE STORY OF NOAH. We've read about the ark,
the animals, the flood. But there's a detail of this story
that is often overlooked. When God had Noah's family
and the animals on board and everything was buttoned
up tight, *God shut the door* (see Genesis 6:9–7:16).

Noah didn't shut it. God shut it—because it was too
late for the rest of humankind to be saved.

Right now, everyone has the chance to call out to
Jesus, but people need to do it while there's still time.
One day, the master of the house will lock the door.

*In living and dying, it's Noah-like
faith that keeps us afloat.*

LINDA PAGE

CAN'T FOOL GOD

*The tax collector stood at a distance and dared
not even lift his eyes to heaven as he prayed.
Instead, he beat his chest in sorrow, saying,
"O God, be merciful to me, for I am a sinner."*

LUKE 18:13

JESUS TOLD A STORY about a Pharisee and a tax collector who came to the Temple to pray (see Luke 18:9-14). The Pharisee's prayer was full of self-praise, while the tax collector humbly confessed his sin. How foolish of the Pharisee to think he could fool God!

No matter how we pray, God sees right through to the naked truth. So why try to puff ourselves up? Jesus tells us to pray as if God knows our hearts better than we do, because he does.

*Lord, help me see my world as you see it. Help
my heart beat with yours. Help me want what
you want—hearts yielded to your will, lives
submitted to your lordship. And, by the way,
I'm ready for you to begin with mine.*

REBECCA MULVANEY

ZACCHAEUS

*The Son of Man came to seek and
save those who are lost.*

LUKE 19:10

ZACCHAEUS, a sinful tax collector, wanted to see Jesus, but he was too short to see over the crowd (see Luke 19:2-8). So Zacchaeus climbed a tree to get a look at the Son of Man. Jesus knew everything about this vertically challenged tax collector. He called Zacchaeus by name and insisted that he would be a guest in Zacchaeus's home. Imagine Zacchaeus's surprise as he scrambled down that tree! Zacchaeus responded to Jesus' love with humility and repentance.

But the onlookers were disgusted and blamed Jesus for going to visit Zacchaeus. Why? Because sometimes people forget that Jesus didn't come to save the self-righteous. He came to save *sinners*.

*Until we look into that mirror and see how far
we've fallen short of God's righteous standard,
we will never see our need for a Savior.*

NANCY GUTHRIE

AUGUST 15

EVEN THE STONES KNOW THE TRUTH

*If [the people] kept quiet, the stones along
the road would burst into cheers!*

LUKE 19:40

AS JESUS TRIUMPHANTLY rode toward Jerusalem, the
crowds spread their coats out on the road. His followers sang his praises and shouted, "Blessings on the King
who comes in the name of the LORD!" This annoyed the
Pharisees, who told Jesus to silence his followers (see
Luke 19:38-39).

Jesus replied, "If they stop praising me, the stones
will take over." This probably baffled the Pharisees, who
didn't understand who Jesus was. But even the stones
along the road knew who Jesus was, because he created
them. Our failure to acknowledge Jesus as Lord does not
take away his lordship. He is King of all creation.

There is a Truth whose mouth will not be shut.
LINDA PAGE

GHOSTS DON'T
HAVE BODIES

*Look at my hands. Look at my feet. You can
see that it's really me. Touch me and make
sure that I am not a ghost, because ghosts
don't have bodies, as you see that I do.*

LUKE 24:39

SOME LIKE TO SUGGEST that those who saw the resurrected Jesus were simply seeing a vision, as if hundreds of people could see the same vision. Some like to suggest that these grieving disciples were only seeing a spirit. But Jesus himself proved these things false when he invited his followers to touch him. Ghosts don't have bodies. Jesus did.

Jesus' disciples did not imagine anything. Jesus was really there. He was as real as reality gets. And he's real to us today. Each day, he invites us to experience his reality.

*Handling his word we feel his
flesh, his bones, and hear
his voice saying our early-morning name.*

LUCI SHAW

OPPORTUNITY TO WORSHIP

*Believe me, dear woman, the time is coming when
it will no longer matter whether you worship
the Father on this mountain or in Jerusalem.*

JOHN 4:21

CHURCH IS A SPECIAL PLACE. It's a place for us to sing together, pray together, and learn together. But the church building is not the only place we can worship. As Jesus explained to the woman at the well, the day would come—and is here now—when people could worship anywhere.

We can worship Jesus in the car, in the woods, in the kitchen. We can worship him as our feet hit the floor in the morning and as we drift off to sleep at night. Today, we are Jesus' temple, and wherever we are, we have an opportunity to worship.

*Close encounters of the divine kind
are daily opportunities. We don't have
to wait for Sunday morning!*

REBECCA MULVANEY

FROM DEATH INTO LIFE

I tell you the truth, those who listen to my message
and believe in God who sent me have eternal life.
They will never be condemned for their sins, but
they have already passed from death into life.

JOHN 5:24

THE MOMENT we start worshiping Jesus, we stop dying.
We listen to Jesus' message, we believe in God, and Jesus
gifts us with eternal life. There has never been, nor will
there ever be, a better plan than that.

Once we accept Jesus' grace, we are permanently rid
of condemnation. Though we will still sin, we can be
forgiven. Though we will still make mistakes, we have
already passed from death into life—life eternal with the
loving Savior who made it possible.

Come home, my soul, to God who waits,
listen to His word, look on His face.

KAY SMITH

COMPASSION AND A FRESH START

Jesus . . . said to the woman, "Where are your accusers? Didn't even one of them condemn you?"
"No, Lord," she said.
And Jesus said, "Neither do I. Go and sin no more."

JOHN 8:10-11

SO MANY OF US CAN relate to the woman caught in sin (see John 8:3-9). The Pharisees had brought her before Jesus for judgment—not because they thought he was qualified, but because they were trying to trick him into saying the wrong thing. But Jesus outsmarted them and changed the course of this woman's life with his words: "He who hasn't sinned can throw the first stone."

No one threw a stone, of course; no one could. The men wandered off as the woman stood up straight. Jesus did not condemn her. Instead he offered her compassion and a fresh start—the same thing he offers us.

Jesus' words proved to the crowd and to this broken woman that, despite her sin and the mistakes she had made, her life mattered.

TRACIE MILES

REMAIN FAITHFUL

*You are truly my disciples if you
remain faithful to my teachings.*

JOHN 8:31

THERE ARE MANY FACETS of discipleship. To follow Jesus,
we must seek him, spend time with him, learn from him,
allow him to change us, love him, allow him to love us,
and show his love to others. But Jesus calls special attention to obedience. To truly follow Jesus, we must remain
faithful to what he has taught us. He doesn't teach us
these things to interfere with our lives. He teaches them
to enrich our lives, to protect us, and to show us his love.

Jesus came to this earth to set sinners free. The only
way to be free of sin is to follow Jesus' teachings. It's all
right there for us in his Word.

*Perfect obedience would be perfect
happiness, if only we had perfect confidence
in the power we were obeying.*

HANNAH WHITALL SMITH

MESS

*Go home to your family, and tell them everything the
Lord has done for you and how merciful he has been.*

MARK 5:19

IMAGINE A MAN, possessed by demons, spending his days
and nights wandering in caves and committing self-harm
(see Mark 5:2-20). His life was a mess. In an instant, Jesus
turned everything around. He sent those spirits into a
herd of pigs and set the man free. The herdsmen fled to
spread the news of this miracle.

The man who had been freed also began to spread the
news. He told everyone in the region about what Jesus
had done. This man probably had moments of wishing
he'd never been in the mess in the first place. But then
the message never would have been spread.

*God is able to take the mess of our past and
turn it into a message. He takes the trials and
tests and turns them into a testimony.*

CHRISTINE CAINE

FRIENDS

I no longer call you slaves, because a master doesn't confide in his slaves. Now you are my friends, since I have told you everything the Father told me.

JOHN 15:15

AT FIRST, JESUS' disciples had a relationship with him that was similar to that of servant (or "slave") and master. But then, the relationship changed. He called them friends—he confided in them and trusted them. They chose to follow and obey him because they knew his way was the best way.

How did the disciples know Jesus this well? Because he put himself on the same level as them. Because he communicated God's truths to them. We too can know Jesus well enough to *choose* to obey him. We too can be his friends.

Jesus needs men and women who make friendship with Him an utmost priority.

GRACE FOX

NOT OUT, BUT THROUGH

I'm not asking you to take them out of the world,
but to keep them safe from the evil one.

JOHN 17:15

THE MOMENT JESUS saves us, why doesn't he just scoop us out of this broken world and whisk us away to paradise? Because we still have work to do. We need to remain in this world for a while so that others might meet (and get to know) Jesus through us. As long as we stay in the world, God has Kingdom work for us to accomplish.

Besides, the Father doesn't need to snatch us out of the fire in order to protect us. He's perfectly capable of protecting us while we're here.

He desires that I remain safe in the heart of his
will—safe from the devil's attempts to trip me
up and snatch me from my Father's grasp.

REBECCA MULVANEY

THE CROWN OF LIFE

*The devil will throw some of you into prison
to test you. You will suffer for ten days. But
if you remain faithful even when facing
death, I will give you the crown of life.*

REVELATION 2:10

PERSECUTION IS HAPPENING all over the world right now. It might even be happening to you or to someone you love. But in these words from Revelation, Jesus gives us some great news. This suffering is temporary. He is well aware of it, and he asks us to remain faithful. And when we do, he will reward us.

*All the way my Savior leads me—
What have I to ask beside?
Can I doubt His tender mercy,
Who through life has been my Guide?
Heav'nly peace, divinest comfort,
Here by faith in Him to dwell!
For I know, whate'er befall me,
Jesus doeth all things well.*

FANNY J. CROSBY

IN SATAN'S CITY

I know that you live in the city where Satan has his throne, yet you have remained loyal to me. You refused to deny me even when Antipas, my faithful witness, was martyred among you there in Satan's city.

REVELATION 2:13

SOMETIMES WE FEEL as though we are living in "Satan's city," as if we are surrounded by people doing the devil's will instead of God's. Sometimes God's people will be persecuted, or even killed. But stay loyal to him. Jesus knows what is happening, and his Kingdom won't be stopped. We won't suffer eternal death: we will be resurrected to spend eternity on the winning side. Jesus won't forget our loyalty.

There is not room for Death,
Nor atom that his might could render void:
Thou—Thou art Being and Breath,
And what Thou art may never be destroyed.

EMILY BRONTË

RIGHT BACK

*All the churches will know that I am
the one who searches out the thoughts
and intentions of every person.*

REVELATION 2:23

IN THE END, everyone will discover that Jesus knows every thought of humankind. He knows when we have our doubts, our selfish moments, and our silent tantrums. That's the bad news. But he also knows when we are sincerely longing for him, when we are so grateful we weep, when we are so humble we can barely speak his name. And that's the very good news.

Jesus knows your thoughts. He hears your heart. He knows how much you love him. And he loves you right back.

*When Jesus looks at me, he sees my heart.
When he looks at you, he sees your heart.
Then from his heart, he responds.*

LINDA PAGE

HANG ON!

I also have a message for the rest of you in Thyatira who have not followed this false teaching ("deeper truths," as they call them—depths of Satan, actually). I will ask nothing more of you except that you hold tightly to what you have until I come.

REVELATION 2:24-25

HANG ON! This life is going to be a bumpy, curvy ride! People will try to knock you off track. They will try to distract you with intellectual rabbit trails, but these "deeper truths" are as shallow as the devil himself.

Don't fall for it. Jesus has given us what we need, and all he asks is that we hold on to what we know—*his* love, *his* grace, *his* commandments—until he comes back for us.

Yea, they shall wax who now are on the wane,
Yea, they shall sing for love when Christ shall come.

CHRISTINA ROSSETTI

SAFE IN HIS ARMS

I give them eternal life, and they will never perish. No one can snatch them away from me, for my Father has given them to me, and he is more powerful than anyone else.

JOHN 10:28-29

JESUS DESCRIBED HIMSELF as the Good Shepherd, and we are his sheep (see John 10:14). We belong to him, and no one can do anything to change that. Jesus is more powerful than anything else in the universe—he *created* the universe.

There is no power, no devil, no fear, no person, no disease, no army that can snatch us out of our Shepherd's loving, protective hands. We are safe with him. We will be safe for eternity. He died on the cross to make it so. If we are afraid, all we need to do to feel brave is to draw closer to the Shepherd.

Our lives are filtered by God's protection and love for us.

DEBBIE ALSDORF

A BRIGHT FUTURE

All who are victorious will become pillars in the Temple of my God, and they will never have to leave it. And I will write on them the name of my God, and they will be citizens in the city of my God—the new Jerusalem that comes down from heaven.

REVELATION 3:12

OUR FUTURE IS too bright to imagine. No matter how good you think it could be, it will be better. In today's verse, Jesus promises believers that we will be *pillars* in the eternal temple and *citizens* in the eternal heavenly city.

Some of us have never won at anything. Some of us have never belonged anywhere. But one day Jesus will make us victorious, and we will permanently belong in heaven. Our future is *brilliant*.

We are in battle . . .
defeat is our name
Triumph
is Yours.

LUCI SHAW

SEEK JUSTICE

God blesses those who hunger and thirst
for justice, for they will be satisfied.

MATTHEW 5:6

CAN YOU REMEMBER the first time you realized life wasn't fair? Maybe you've been there when a child discovered this sad truth. The world *isn't* fair. But God always is. He is always fair, always just, always right.

This makes it difficult for us who live simultaneously in this world and in God's heavenly Kingdom. But in today's verse Jesus promises that we will be blessed when we hunger and thirst for justice, when we work to make situations fair for those who are being treated unfairly. We may think we can't change things, but we can do one small thing for one person, and that will be noticed by God.

It is enough for us to seek Thy Kingdom and its
justice. All the rest will be added unto us.

JEANNE-FRANÇOISE DE CHANTAL

BLESSED ARE THE PERSECUTED

God blesses those who are persecuted for doing right, for the Kingdom of Heaven is theirs.

MATTHEW 5:10

MOST OF US do not directly equate persecution with glory. Most of us do not wish for an opportunity to suffer or to die for Jesus' name. Yet so many before us have done just this. So many are dying for Jesus' sake right now.

Jesus taught his followers that these persecuted souls will be blessed with the Kingdom of Heaven. They will experience an eternal glory the magnitude of which diminishes even the most intense suffering on earth.

And behold now through the Holy Ghost, I am sprinkled with heavenly dew! The furnace grows cold at my side, and the flame is divided asunder, and the heat of the fire poured back on to those by whom it was kindled.

AGNES OF ROME

MERCY TRUMPS SACRIFICE

Go and learn the meaning of this Scripture:
"I want you to show mercy, not offer sacrifices."

MATTHEW 9:13

JESUS QUOTED HOSEA 6:6 to the Pharisees, who should have known the verse but certainly weren't acting as if they did. They thought that observing religious practices such as sacrifices was all God cared about. But God cares more about repentant hearts.

What good is it to act however we want and then say we're sorry? Our hearts don't change, our behavior doesn't change, and the sorry quickly loses its meaning. God doesn't want us to control our own lives and then apologize for the wreckage. He wants us to give him control of our lives so he can lead us in his righteous ways.

God's glory in our lives has little to do with our
sacrifice and everything to do with our surrender.

ALISA HOPE WAGNER

THEY CANNOT TOUCH YOUR SOUL

Don't be afraid of those who want to kill your body; they cannot touch your soul. Fear only God, who can destroy both soul and body in hell.

MATTHEW 10:28

SOMETIMES JESUS' CHALLENGES seem impossibly tall. Don't fear someone who wants to kill us? But it is true, of course, that the power of the most powerful enemy we could possibly face is trifling compared to God's infinite, eternal power. We know this truth and—with practice— we can put it into action. No matter what we face in life, God is bigger, God is stronger, and there is nothing else worthy of our fear.

Be Thou the captain of our souls! Then if poverty comes we shall not be so poor and if sorrow comes we shall not be so sad, and if death comes we shall not be afraid.

EVANGELINE BOOTH

SHOW ME

O Father, Lord of heaven and earth, thank
you for hiding these things from those who
think themselves wise and clever, and
for revealing them to the childlike.

MATTHEW 11:25

HAVE YOU EVER caught yourself feeling pretty smart? If you have, there's a good chance that feeling was quickly followed up by some humbling circumstance orchestrated by God—because we humans are oh, so silly when thinking about our own power. It is only through supernatural revelation from Jesus that we are able to understand anything. And we get this supernatural insight only when we come to Jesus like children, pleading, "Show me!"

We read without comprehending unless Thou
open our understanding: give us intelligence.

CHRISTINA ROSSETTI

GREATER THAN THE TEMPLE

*I tell you, there is one here who is
even greater than the Temple!*

MATTHEW 12:6

IT'S DIFFICULT FOR us to imagine the gravity of these words, because we don't live in the time of the Temple. To us, God is everywhere: in creation, in our homes, in our hearts. But to the immediate audience for Jesus' words, God lived in the Temple. The Temple was the center of their religious culture; it was the focal point of their faith; it was their identity.

We have it so much easier. We don't need to go to any physical location to be close to God, thanks to Jesus, who is greater than the Temple. He changed everything when he came to earth, and we get to reap the benefits every single day.

*Thus shall I rest, unmov'd by all alarms,
Secure within the temple of thine arms.*

ANNA LAETITIA BARBAULD

SOVEREIGN GRACE

*He will send out his angels with the mighty
blast of a trumpet, and they will gather his
chosen ones from all over the world—from
the farthest ends of the earth and heaven.*

MATTHEW 24:31

JUST IMAGINE the moment when Jesus returns. What will
that trumpet sound like? How many angels will there be?
What will they look like? Will we even see them, or will
they just whisk us away in an instant?

We are his chosen ones, and he is going to gather us
to him one final time. Then we will be with him forever,
and nothing will ever take us away from him.

*Among thy saints let me be found,
Whene'er the archangel's trump shall sound,
To see thy smiling face;
Then loudest of the throng I'll sing,
While heaven's resounding mansions ring
With shouts of sovereign grace.*

SELINA, COUNTESS OF HUNTINGDON

WE CAN'T KNOW

No one knows the day or hour when these things will happen, not even the angels in heaven or the Son himself. Only the Father knows.

MATTHEW 24:36

WE WOMEN LIKE to be in the know. We like to figure things out, know what's coming, and be prepared. But no matter how many numbers we crunch, the timing of Jesus' return is one equation we're just not going to solve. And God planned it that way.

He must want us to invest our energies in bigger and better things. We've just got to trust that when the time is right, God will send Jesus back to earth. It won't be too soon or too late. His timing is always perfect.

Help me to be not too curious in prying into those secret things that are known only to thee, O God, nor too rash in censuring what I do not understand.

SUSANNA WESLEY

THE HEART'S TREASURY

A good person produces good things from the
treasury of a good heart, and an evil person produces
evil things from the treasury of an evil heart.
What you say flows from what is in your heart.

LUKE 6:45

IT IS UNNERVING to think that Jesus hears every word we say and knows every thought we think. He hears us nagging at our husband, snapping at our children, the things we say in traffic, the things we mutter under our breath.

All these words originate in our hearts. If we're saying things that we know won't make Jesus proud, we can get to the bottom of the issue by examining our hearts—hearts only his love can change.

Let it be given me each hour today what I
shall say, and grant me the wisdom of a loving
heart that I may say the right thing rightly.

LUCY H. M. SOULSBY

GOD'S RIGHT HAND

*From now on the Son of Man will be seated
in the place of power at God's right hand.*

LUKE 22:69

WHEN SOMEONE IS PLACED at a leader's right hand, they gain equal footing and equal power with that leader. Jesus said he would be "at God's right hand," meaning, essentially, that he was the same as God.

What good news this is for us!

Jesus said, "From now on." It wasn't a temporary arrangement. Jesus is still there, at God's right hand. He has the power of God, and he's using it on our behalf!

*O Lord Jesus Christ! I adore Thee restored to life
among the dead, ascending into Heaven and
seating Thyself at the right hand of Thy Father:
I implore Thee to make me worthy to follow
Thee thither, and to be presented to Thee.*

CATHERINE DE RICCI

STAIRWAY TO HEAVEN

*I tell you the truth, you will all see heaven
open and the angels of God going up and
down on the Son of Man, the one who is the
stairway between heaven and earth.*

JOHN 1:51

JESUS PROMISED his disciple Nathanael that he would
see Jesus surrounded by the angels. Imagine Nathanael's
response to such a claim, to such an image—Jesus as a set
of stairs stretching into the sky!

Jesus does connect earth and heaven. He opened up
the Kingdom of Heaven to us. The angels minister to
Jesus and, through him, minister to us. Jesus is the true
stairway to heaven. He is the only way to get there.

*There let the way appear
Steps unto heaven;
All that Thou sendest me
In mercy given;
Angels to beckon me
Nearer, my God, to Thee,
Nearer to Thee.*

SARAH FLOWER ADAMS

SEPTEMBER 10

SPIRITUAL LIFE

*I assure you, no one can enter the Kingdom of
God without being born of water and the Spirit.
Humans can reproduce only human life, but
the Holy Spirit gives birth to spiritual life.*

JOHN 3:5-6

THERE'S A REASON Jesus used the words "born again"
(John 3:3) to describe salvation. Our spirits are inert within
us until the moment we choose to follow Jesus, and then
our spirits spring to life as the Holy Spirit flows into us to
establish his residence. Because of him, everything changes.

Some things change quickly—we go through great
growth spurts. Some changes take time—like a thin tree
struggling to add a single ring. But make no mistake.
The Holy Spirit is growing us spiritually, and we can do
nothing worthwhile apart from his power.

*And every virtue we possess,
And every victory won,
And every thought of holiness,
Are His alone.*

HARRIET AUBER

EVERYONE

*Everyone who asks, receives. Everyone
who seeks, finds. And to everyone who
knocks, the door will be opened.*

MATTHEW 7:8

JESUS DOES NOT TURN people away. He is giving everyone
on this earth a chance to take his free gift of life. If they
seek, they will find. If they knock, he will open the door.
Isn't this fantastic news!

Jesus isn't off limits to anyone. He's for the woman
who sleeps in the alley because she has nowhere else to
go. He's for the woman who walks by without seeing that
woman in the alley. He's for the child living with autism.
He's for the mom raising that child. He's for the convict,
the victim, and the warden. He's for you.

*Climb into the surety of My heart and raise
your standards of prayer, for I have something
better for you today than you've asked for.*

MARIE CHAPIAN

BIG DEAL

Those who speak for themselves want glory only for themselves, but a person who seeks to honor the one who sent him speaks truth, not lies.

JOHN 7:18

JESUS SAID, "This isn't about *me*. This is about the one who sent me." Jesus didn't try to glorify himself—his purpose was to honor the Father.

Our culture puts a lot of value on being a big deal. We are trained to believe that our worth lies in applause, in promotions, in getting the credit. We feel validated when we get good reviews, public praise, and our name in lights. But none of these things are truly significant unless they glorify God.

We want *God* to be the big deal. Our only real value lies in him, and that's something worth celebrating.

O my God, let me walk in the way of love which knoweth not how to seek self in anything whatsoever.

GERTRUDE MORE

ONE FLOCK

I have other sheep, too, that are not in this sheepfold.
I must bring them also. They will listen to my voice,
and there will be one flock with one shepherd.

JOHN 10:16

THE BIBLE RECORDS hundreds of statements straight from
Jesus' lips. Yet none of them tell us which denomination
to join. Think for a moment about how much energy
believers spend joining churches, leaving churches, *split-
ting* churches. Think about how much time we spend
arguing tiny points of doctrine and turning up our noses
at the way they do things at the church down the road.

Now imagine how much we could accomplish for
Jesus if we simply worked together—even when we are
different, even when we disagree. The same Jesus saves
us all.

Family of families,
Church of many churches we;
One in soul, one voice shall rise,
Morn and eve, O God, to Thee.

EMMA WILLARD

DIDN'T I TELL YOU?

*Didn't I tell you that you would see
God's glory if you believe?*

JOHN 11:40

LAZARUS'S SISTER MARTHA wasn't quite sure what was going on. Her brother had been dead for four days, and then here came Jesus telling her to open the tomb (see John 11:17-39). Surely this couldn't be a good idea! Yet, Jesus asked her, "Didn't I tell you that you would see God's glory if you believe?"

He says the same thing to us each and every day. When we open our hearts, our minds, and our eyes to it, we see God's glory everywhere. All we have to do is believe.

Jesus gave Lazarus new life. He gives us new life every day. And in our own transformation, we see God's glory up close and personal.

*Into my soul Thy glory pours like
sunlight, edged with gold.*

MECHTHILD OF MAGDEBURG

LIFTED UP

When I am lifted up from the earth,
I will draw everyone to myself.

JOHN 12:32

JESUS FORETOLD the way that he would die: he would be "lifted up from the earth" on a wooden cross. Yet through his death, he would draw souls to himself from all over the world and throughout time.

There's also a metaphor here. Other people are drawn to Jesus when his believers lift him up. People are less likely to be drawn to him when we keep him on a dusty shelf, buried in history and tradition. But when we lift him up with praise and reverence, when we give him the glory he's due, people will be drawn to that—they'll be drawn to *him*.

Upon that cross of Jesus
mine eye at times can see
the very dying form of One
who suffered there for me.

ELIZABETH C. CLEPHANE

WASH EACH OTHER'S FEET

Since I, your Lord and Teacher, have washed your feet, you ought to wash each other's feet.

JOHN 13:14

SINCE JESUS FIRST taught us to wash each other's feet, many believers have maintained a literal foot-washing tradition. Missionaries working among people who live barefoot often find this is a viable way to connect to people's hearts. We don't have to literally wash one another's feet to follow this command. We do, however, need to serve one another as Jesus served us. We need to volunteer to do the menial tasks—and then do them quietly, with love, without expecting praise.

Did he not even stoop to wash the feet of His disciples, to teach them a lesson of affectionate humility! And shall not I, a poor sinful creature, rejoice to be able to administer any comfort or assistance to the meanest of His servants?

ANNE STEELE

WALKING IN DARKNESS

Those who walk in the darkness
cannot see where they are going.

JOHN 12:35

KIDS LOVE TO PLAY while blindfolded because it's fun to smash into things. It's not so fun, however, when your body has finished growing and isn't quite as pliable as it once was. Whether you're walking through the forest and your flashlight dies or you're trying to find your way to a midnight snack, walking in darkness leads to bumps and bruises.

People without Jesus live like this. They have no light to guide them. And they have the scars to show for it. Let us do what we can to shine the light of Jesus into their lives.

But we thank Thee, O God, that the light of Heaven
has illumined our pathway and that Thou hast
given unto us the light that underlies living
power to sustain and to uphold at all times.

E. T. CAWDRY

FITTING IN

The world would love you as one of its own if you belonged to it, but you are no longer part of the world. I chose you to come out of the world, so it hates you.

SOME PEOPLE SPEND their whole lives trying to fit in. They just never seem to click with the people around them. But Jesus tells us this is normal for Christians. We *aren't supposed to fit in.* We *are* different. Jesus has pulled us out of this world and shown us a different way of living.

But things *will* click later when we are all together in paradise with Jesus, who will make sure we all fit in.

As for me, what matters it what men think of me, or what they make me suffer, since they cannot separate me from that Saviour whose name is engraven in the very bottom of my heart?

JEANNE-MARIE GUYON

SANCTIFICATION

*Make them holy by your truth; teach
them your word, which is truth.*

JOHN 17:17

JESUS PRAYED THESE words for his disciples, knowing the
only way they would become the people God created
them to be was through the power of God's Word.

God has chosen us, and he sets us apart as *his*. Then
the Holy Spirit works on us our whole lives to get us
closer to the people God created us to be. This can be
painful, or it can be exhilarating. Sometimes it can be
both. As we get to know the truth through God's Word,
we become more and more like him, closer and closer
to holy.

*So teach me, I humbly beseech Thee, Thy word,
and so straighten me with Thy grace that I
may feed Thy people with a faithful and a true
heart, and rule them prudently with power.*

QUEEN ELIZABETH I

WITHOUT SEEING ME

You believe because you have seen me. Blessed
are those who believe without seeing me.

JOHN 20:29

AFTER THE RESURRECTION, people *saw* Jesus with their own eyes. They were able to talk to him face to face. They were able to eat with him. They were able to touch his wounds. Thomas, the disciple who doubted, didn't believe Jesus had risen until he saw him for himself—but all the believers who would come after Jesus had ascended to heaven would have to believe by faith alone.

We will probably never see Jesus in this lifetime. Yet we still believe. So we are blessed! Today we believe without seeing. But one day in heaven, the truth will be right before our eyes, as plain as perpetual day.

Lo! now what I have believed, that I see;
what I have hoped, that I now hold; what
I have desired, that I embrace.

AGNES OF ROME

MY WITNESSES

*You will receive power when the Holy
Spirit comes upon you. And you will be
my witnesses, telling people about me
everywhere—in Jerusalem, throughout Judea,
in Samaria, and to the ends of the earth.*

ACTS 1:8

JESUS CHARGED his small band of misfit followers with
spreading his gospel all over the world. This was no small
challenge! But they did a great job, by the power of the
Holy Spirit, because it spread like wildfire. It even made
its way to us.

By the power of the Holy Spirit, may the gospel of
Jesus continue to spread through us, until every soul on
the planet has heard.

*Give me, O Lord, so strong a voice that when I call
Thee Love, I shall be heard from East to West, and in
all parts of the world and in the depths of Hell, so that
Thou mayest be known and adored as True Love.*

MARY MAGDALENE DEI PAZZI

ON YOUR FEET!

Get to your feet! For I have appeared to you to appoint you as my servant and witness.

ACTS 26:16

IF JESUS APPEARED to us in the middle of a road, we would probably fall down too, just like Paul did (see Acts 26:12-15). And how impossible it probably sounded to him when Jesus commanded, "Get up!" Yet, that's what Jesus says to us, too.

Once we have a meaningful encounter with Jesus, once we realize that he truly is the Son of God, once we fall before him in reverence, he doesn't waste any time in saying, "Now get up. You are my servant and witness. I have things for you to do." And then he sets us free to do them.

Reign Thou and let me be the captive, for my soul covets no other freedom.

TERESA OF AVILA

THE FIRST AND THE LAST

Don't be afraid!
I am the First and the Last.

REVELATION 1:17

BY SAYING THAT he is the First and the Last, Jesus says that he is God. He has always been and he always will be. He was here before Creation, and he will be here when this world passes away.

What does this mean to us? That we have absolutely nothing to be afraid of. Jesus not only has seen it all, but he also saw it all before it happened. Our lives are completely in his control. In the face of such eternal power, all that we fear—our wars, our pain, our sickness, our grief—are only blips on his screen. And he has given us the honor of including us in his eternity, where we can live fearlessly forever.

Stretching those wounded Hands out to our aid;
Telling us tenderly, "Be not afraid!"

DORA SIGERSON SHORTER

KEEP KEEPING ON

*I know all the things you do. I have seen
your love, your faith, your service, and
your patient endurance. And I can see your
constant improvement in all these things.*

REVELATION 2:19

HAVE YOU EVER LOOKED around at the broken world and become daunted by how much there is to do? It can seem like we work all day long and never make a dent. We may feel as though we just can't do enough for Jesus with our measly efforts.

Jesus sees you. He sees the work you do, no matter how tiny the task. And he sees not only the things you do but also your *improvement*. He sees your growth, even if you don't.

You can just keep keeping on, knowing that he is watching.

*The more I love Thee, it seems the less I love
Thee, because I want to love Thee more.*

FRANCES XAVIER CABRINI

THE AMEN

*This is the message from the one who is
the Amen—the faithful and true witness,
the beginning of God's new creation.*

REVELATION 3:14

AMEN! So be it! Isn't that the truth! Jesus is all these expressions and more. He is the beginning of God's new creation. When he came to earth, he brought with him a new way of existing. He changed everything, and we get to reap the benefits. And there are still changes to come. One day we will live in a new city where he will reign. One day we will sit at his feet in complete peace.

*We are of yesterday and know nothing. But Thy
boundless mind comprehends, at one view, all
things, past, present and future, and as Thou
dost see all things, Thou does best understand
what is good and proper for each individual
and for me, with relation to both worlds.*

SUSANNA WESLEY

WHITE GARMENTS

*Buy white garments from me so you will not
be shamed by your nakedness, and ointment
for your eyes so you will be able to see.*

REVELATION 3:18

THIS VERSE IS PART of Jesus' letter to the church in
Laodicea, a city known for its production of black wool
and eye salve. What apt metaphors it uses for the condi-
tions we trade in for Jesus. We take off the itchy black
wool of sin and put on the soft, spotless garments of his
forgiveness. We put his ointment on our eyes, and they
open to his way of being.

Why wear black when we can wear his white? Why
be blind when he can make us see?

Fain would I be cheerful, and sing as I go,
Uplifting Thy praises through darkness and dawn;
Fain wear a white robe, not the garment of woe,
And joyously, blithely, and gayly go on.

MARGARET E. SANGSTER

LOVING DISCIPLINE

I correct and discipline everyone I love. So be diligent and turn from your indifference.

REVELATION 3:19

OUR CHILDREN don't enjoy being disciplined. Yet they seem to take it better than we do. It's as if they understand we are disciplining them out of love. So why do we make such a stink when Jesus disciplines us? A lack of discipline would mean a lack of love, and we don't want that!

Let us not only tolerate his discipline but also embrace it. Let us say thank you when we go through those rough patches designed to train us and strengthen us. Jesus wouldn't teach us these lessons if we didn't need them. Let us be diligent in our training, not indifferent, and let's work to please him the way children work to please the parents they love.

Thou knowest better what is good for me than I do.

LADY JANE GREY

A STUDENT OF JESUS

As Jesus was walking along, he saw a man named
Matthew sitting at his tax collector's booth.
"Follow me and be my disciple," Jesus said to
him. So Matthew got up and followed him.

MATTHEW 9:9

CAN YOU IMAGINE Matthew's surprise? He was sitting there, doing his daily thing, when Jesus stopped in front of him. "Follow me," Jesus said.

At some point, Jesus has whispered to your heart also: "Follow me." Many of us, when we hear this call, stand up and respond. But Matthew didn't just follow Jesus around. From that day on, he became a student. He listened to Jesus' teachings. He watched his miracles. He served others alongside Jesus.

We, too, can be students of Jesus. He has so much to teach us.

The word disciple means "pupil" or "learner."
We will never cease to be God's children,
but when we cease learning and being
teachable, we are no longer disciples.

BETH MOORE

NO TESTS NECESSARY

*The Scriptures also say, "You must
not test the LORD your God."*

MATTHEW 4:7

JESUS QUOTED Deuteronomy 6:16, reminding us of an important principle: we mere, small earthlings have no business testing the God of the universe. Yet it's tempting to sometimes say, "If you're real, just prove it" or "If you're here, give me a sign."

God isn't in the business of passing our tests. He is the Almighty Father—he doesn't have to prove himself to anyone or anything. And he doesn't want to give us proof *so that* we'll believe. He wants us to believe and *then* receive the proof. And that proof most often happens in our hearts, where the faith lives.

*God doesn't bless us so that we'll know
He's faithful—we trust in His faithfulness
and then discover His blessings.*

KARON PHILLIPS GOODMAN

DON'T MISS OUT!

Don't misunderstand why I have come. I did not come to abolish the law of Moses or the writings of the prophets. No, I came to accomplish their purpose.

MATTHEW 5:17

IMAGINE STUDIOUSLY viewing a long, complicated movie and then refusing to watch the ending. That's sort of what the religious leaders of Jesus' time did. They knew the history, but they refused to open their eyes (and hearts) to the climax of the story.

Everything—from Creation through history to their present time—pointed to Jesus. The very law these leaders held so dear was given to point toward humankind's need for a Savior. Yet they refused to acknowledge that. Oh, what love and freedom they missed out on—the same love and freedom people miss out on today when they refuse to acknowledge who Jesus is.

Friend, Jesus wants you to live and walk in the freedom of the cross.

WENDY BLIGHT

NOT EVEN THE SMALLEST DETAIL

I tell you the truth, until heaven and earth disappear, not even the smallest detail of God's law will disappear until its purpose is achieved.

MATTHEW 5:18

GOD'S LAW was not arbitrary. Every rule he gave was given to protect his people—physically, socially, mentally, and spiritually. And not a single letter of his law would go away until it had accomplished the purpose he intended it to.

It is the same for his commands for us today. His Word serves a purpose—to help us, to grow us, to protect us. God knows the details. He created them.

God is interested in the tiniest things in the world. He cares about us and what we consider important. He gives us the desires of our hearts. He completes what He begins. He knows us by name.

LUCI SWINDOLL

THE TASK OF TEACHING

*If you ignore the least commandment and teach
others to do the same, you will be called the
least in the Kingdom of Heaven. But anyone
who obeys God's laws and teaches them will
be called great in the Kingdom of Heaven.*

MATTHEW 5:19

CONSIDER THE GRAVITY of being a teacher! It's not a task
to be taken lightly, yet so many of us become teachers
whether we mean to or not. We are mothers, aunts, grand-
mothers, Sunday school teachers, VBS volunteers. Let's
make sure we take our job—and God's Word—seriously.

*When my doctrine is purer and the truth I teach
more scorching, the worldly will abandon me,
but Thou wilt then press me against Thy heart,
Thy heart which knew so well the meaning of
loneliness and abandonment. Only in Thy look
shall I see the sweetness of approbation.*

GABRIELA MISTRAL

RIGHTEOUSNESS THROUGH JESUS

*I warn you—unless your righteousness is
better than the righteousness of the teachers
of religious law and the Pharisees, you will
never enter the Kingdom of Heaven!*

MATTHEW 5:20

JESUS WAS NOT SUGGESTING we need to be perfect. In fact, he was pointing out that *outward* perfection really doesn't accomplish much at all. Even if we worked as hard as the Pharisees, who were expert rule followers, we would still come up short.

The truth is that the only kind of righteousness that will get us into the Kingdom of Heaven is the righteousness that comes through the blood of Jesus. This isn't something we can earn; it is a gift we have to ask for.

*Lord, for these simple things I plead . . .
that I be dedicated to the truth and
clothed in the fire of righteousness.*

WILMA CURTIS

JESUS' KIND OF KINDNESS

If you are kind only to your friends, how are you different from anyone else? Even pagans do that.

MATTHEW 5:47

YOU'VE PROBABLY ENJOYED friendships with some caring, generous people who were not followers of Jesus. Often these people are motivated by friendship itself. They want people to like them, to spend time with them, to be kind to them, and to help them through life, so they show the kind of kindness they want to receive.

This isn't the kind of kindness Jesus presents. He wants us to show kindness out of love—*his* love. He wants us to show kindness with no expectations.

The core of the Christian heart is love. It walks with a humbleness toward others—a gentle knowing that we're all the same at the foot of the cross of Jesus.

KENISHA BETHEA

JUDGE NOT

Do not judge others, and you will not be judged.

MATTHEW 7:1

WE ARE SUPPOSED to be wise about the decisions *we* make. We are supposed to exercise sound judgment in *our* lives. But Jesus doesn't want us running around judging *others'* lives. This is not our job, and it probably won't attract many people to the gospel.

Instead, Jesus wants us to show the same compassion to others that he has shown to us. He wants us to show the same mercy that he has shown to us. We don't have to condone other people's sin, but we can still be gentle listeners who lead them toward a Savior, and we can do this without harsh judgment.

We are all sinners. We all need Jesus. We can leave the judging up to him.

Guilt is darkness; mercy is light.

LISA BEVERE

OCTOBER 6

WOLVES IN SHEEP'S CLOTHING

Beware of false prophets who come disguised as harmless sheep but are really vicious wolves.

MATTHEW 7:15

THIS VERSE IS a little scary! But it happens all the time. The enemy places people in positions of authority where they can lie for him. And these people are often successful because they mix some truth in with their lies. They twist Jesus' truth in the hopes that we won't really notice it's not coming out right.

We can defend ourselves from these wolves by spending time talking directly to Jesus and by spending time in his Word. If someone says something that doesn't align with Jesus' truth, then we need to distance ourselves from that person, who just might be a wolf!

Satan's goal is to deafen us to God's voice so that we embrace his thinking as easily and naturally as if it were God's very own.

SHELLY BEACH

THE HARVEST

The harvest is great, but the workers are few. So
pray to the Lord who is in charge of the harvest;
ask him to send more workers into his fields.

MATTHEW 9:37-38

MISSIONS ORGANIZATIONS share that there are millions
of people in this world who haven't yet heard the gospel.
And these people aren't necessarily living in developing
countries. They may be living next door.

We can all be workers in God's fields. We can also all
be prayer warriors. As we are working to share the gospel,
we can pray for others who are doing the same, and we
can pray that God would send more people into his fields.

O join this mighty army
There's a battle to be won;
Let us now put in the sickle.
For the harvest time has come;
Countless multitudes are waiting
Just to hear of God's own Son.
His army marches on!

JULIA WARD HOWE

NOTHING IS SECRET

Don't be afraid of those who threaten you.
For the time is coming when everything
that is covered will be revealed, and all that
is secret will be made known to all.

MATTHEW 10:26

"DON'T BE AFRAID of those who threaten you." That's easier said than done, especially when we live in a world where criminals get away with their crimes and get rich while they're at it. But nothing is ever really secret. God knows everything that happens, and each of us will be held accountable. Until then, we can have peace in remembering that God is just.

Help us boldly to tackle every invasion of fear. We
hurl it from us, cast it at Your feet, and force ourselves
to be quiet. Then Your Creative and Holy Spirit
somehow, gradually, links us to that Peace that the
world can't give and the world can't take away.

MURIEL LESTER

SOMEONE EVEN STRONGER

Who is powerful enough to enter the house
of a strong man and plunder his goods? Only
someone even stronger—someone who could
tie him up and then plunder his house.

MATTHEW 12:29

SATAN IS STRONG, but his strength is paltry compared to Jesus' power. So we who follow Jesus have nothing to fear and nothing to worry about. Jesus is strong enough to bind Satan and rescue the children who are living under his control. There is no reason for us to let Satan have any authority over our lives. We serve a mighty King, a King of unmatched power. And he fights for us.

The hardest part about letting God fight
your battle is that He sometimes waits until
the eleventh hour so you will have no doubt
of where the power is coming from.

STORMIE OMARTIAN

BLASPHEMY AGAINST THE HOLY SPIRIT

I tell you, every sin and blasphemy can be forgiven—except blasphemy against the Holy Spirit, which will never be forgiven.

MATTHEW 12:31

JESUS WAS DRIVING out demons, and the religious leaders accused him of being in league with Satan (see Matthew 12:22-24). Jesus was doing things under the power of the Holy Spirit, and his critics accused him of doing things under the power of the devil. Not only did they not give the Holy Spirit credit for his power, but they gave the credit to Satan!

We can avoid this sin by recognizing the power of the Holy Spirit and by allowing that power to enter us and change us from the inside out.

Allow yourself to be led by the Spirit of God. That Spirit will unerringly conduct you to the end purpose for which your soul was created . . . the enjoyment of God.

JEANNE-MARIE GUYON

THE SIGN OF JONAH

*Only an evil, adulterous generation would demand
a miraculous sign; but the only sign I will give
them is the sign of the prophet Jonah. For as Jonah
was in the belly of the great fish for three days
and three nights, so will the Son of Man be in the
heart of the earth for three days and three nights.*

MATTHEW 12:39-40

PEOPLE WANTED to see some miraculous proof that Jesus
was who he said he was. Ironically, he gave them the most
amazing proof of all: the Resurrection. And still some of
them didn't believe.

Jonah had an amazing story to tell. The leaders of
Jesus' time believed it. Yet they failed to believe that Jesus
had risen, even after he promised he would.

*The mightiest signs and wonders cannot change
our hearts! Only the Spirit of God can do that!*

LYNN ANDERSON

THE FLOODGATES

*The people of Nineveh will stand up against
this generation on judgment day and condemn
it, for they repented of their sins at the
preaching of Jonah. Now someone greater than
Jonah is here—but you refuse to repent.*

MATTHEW 12:41

JESUS' IMMEDIATE AUDIENCE would have known Jonah's story well. He was a prophet, a hero. The religious leaders of Jesus' time would have understood what Jesus meant when he spoke of the evil city of Nineveh, whose people fell to their knees in shame before an almighty God.

Yet the religious leaders refused to understand who Jesus was, no matter how much he told them or how much he showed them. Perhaps they were simply unwilling to repent, and repentance is a necessary first step to seeing Jesus for who he is.

*Repentance always opens the
floodgates to healing and love.*

DEE BRESTIN & KATHY TROCCOLI

THE CORNERSTONE

Didn't you ever read this in the Scriptures?
"The stone that the builders rejected has
now become the cornerstone. This is the
LORD's doing, and it is wonderful to see."

MATTHEW 21:42

JESUS WAS QUOTING Psalm 118 and applying the prophecy to himself. The builders, the Jewish leaders, rejected the most important part of the universe—the Son of God. This Son would become the cornerstone, the most important part of the foundation of God's Kingdom. And Jesus said it's "wonderful to see"! As the psalmist had predicted hundreds of years before, it was all part of God's plan.

Without a cornerstone, a building can't stand against weather, enemies, or time. Without Jesus, religion is pointless. Without Jesus, faith crumbles. Without Jesus, our lives have no stability, no endurance, no future.

Foundations to be reliable must
always be unshakable.

HANNAH WHITALL SMITH

INVITE EVERYONE YOU SEE!

*Go out to the street corners and
invite everyone you see.*

MATTHEW 22:9

JESUS USES A PARABLE to describe the Kingdom of Heaven (see Matthew 22:2-9). In his story, the king (God) prepares a great feast for his son and invites all his people (the Jews). But the Jews ignore his invitation. So God sends his messengers back out to invite everyone in sight. That's us!

We can place ourselves in this parable. Imagine just being your poor old self on the side of the street and the king's messenger pops out of the castle and says, "Come to the feast! Come as you are! You don't need to do anything! It's all ready!"

*God showed me He isn't in the business of dividing
a sliver of opportunity among His children:
He's in the business of making a bigger pie!*

GLYNNIS WHITWER

ELATION OR MOURNING

*Then at last, the sign that the Son of Man is coming
will appear in the heavens, and there will be deep
mourning among all the peoples of the earth.
And they will see the Son of Man coming on the
clouds of heaven with power and great glory.*

MATTHEW 24:30

IF WE TAKE THIS VERSE literally, which most believers do,
Jesus is describing quite the spectacle. Imagine you're on
your morning commute and the skies split open, and
suddenly the whole world can see Jesus' face. Or you're
just about to doze off and it comes on the news.

Everyone is going to react—either with divine relief
and elation or with terror and mourning. Let's hope there
is more of the former.

> *I will watch for the Lord;*
> *I'll meet Him in the air.*
> *I will watch for the Lord;*
> *I'm on the edge of my chair.*

FAYE SMITH

HIS WORDS WILL NEVER DISAPPEAR

*Heaven and earth will disappear, but
my words will never disappear.*

MATTHEW 24:35

THE EARTH AS WE KNOW it will eventually come to an end. Even heaven in its current state will disappear. But Jesus never changes. He was the same gentle, loving King before the universe began, and he will be the same when he rules his eternal Kingdom.

Because Jesus never changes, his Word never changes. Even when people try to twist it, water it down, or abolish it, it won't change. So when the changes of this life keep us bouncing around and we're just trying to stay afloat, we can turn to the Word for stability, assurance, and life.

*I want to bathe my soul in Thy infinity,
like the workingmen who
plunge into the surf to shed the dust
and heat of their bodies.*

A MOTHER IN AFRICA

OCTOBER 17

YOUR INHERITANCE

The King will say to those on his right, "Come, you who are blessed by my Father, inherit the Kingdom prepared for you from the creation of the world."

MATTHEW 25:34

JESUS DESCRIBED the final judgment, which will be terrifying for many people (see Matthew 25:31-46). But those of us who belong to the Good Shepherd have nothing to worry about. While we'll probably still be in reverential fear, we will be placed on Jesus' right, and then we will be invited into the Kingdom he has prepared for us.

It's easy to feel immensely loved as we read about our glorious, unmerited future, a future planned for us since before the beginning.

Riches I heed not, nor man's empty praise,
Thou mine inheritance, now and always;
Thou and Thou only, first in my heart,
High King of heaven, my treasure Thou art.

ELEANOR HENRIETTA HULL &

MARY ELIZABETH BYRNE

OCTOBER 18

THIS WOMAN'S DEED

I tell you the truth, wherever the Good News is preached throughout the world, this woman's deed will be remembered and discussed.

MATTHEW 26:13

THE WOMAN WITH the alabaster jar probably didn't know what a profound role she was playing in the gospel (see Matthew 26:6-12). She surely didn't know that she would be included in God's Word, that she would be studied in theology classes and admired for her devotion. Yet she is.

We have no idea what God has planned for us. He doesn't tell us, because we don't need to know. We just need to go about our daily lives, being worshipful and obedient, and let God take care of the big picture.

As God's children, our lives unfold daily like pages in a book. Each circumstance is a different chapter. Each page is a new opportunity to live out God's plan for us.

THELMA WELLS

THE PRACTICAL DETAILS

I feel sorry for these people. They have been here with me for three days, and they have nothing left to eat.

MARK 8:2

JESUS IS FULLY GOD and is fully aware of all things divine at all times. But this doesn't mean he is aloof from the practical details of our lives. Quite the opposite! When we are hungry, he knows it, and he cares. When we are thirsty, tired, sick, or sore, Jesus knows, and he cares.

We should never feel as though anything is too small for his love. He is always just a prayer away, no matter how mundane our need.

The Gospel accounts show Him with a passion for helping those in trouble. He has not changed. The minute we need saving from anything, He stands ready in His role as Saviour.

CATHERINE MARSHALL

THE GOD OF THE LIVING

He is the God of the living, not the dead.
You have made a serious error.

MARK 12:27

JESUS WAS TALKING to the Sadducees, religious leaders who did not believe in life after death (see Mark 12:18). You probably know people today who make this same "serious error." But God's *not* dead, and his people aren't either—at least not permanently. Our bodies will be resurrected, and we will live eternally with him.

Followers of Jesus pin all their hopes on his resurrection. Without it, Jesus is just another dead prophet. But he's no longer in the tomb. He is the living God of the universe, alive in heaven and alive in us.

The evidence is all around us. Jesus *changes* people. He breathes new life into souls, and one day he will bring new life to our bodies as well.

Nothing—nothing!—is too far gone
that your God cannot resurrect it.

PRISCILLA SHIRER

CONSTANT SEEKING

*Why did you need to search? . . . Didn't you
know that I must be in my Father's house?*

LUKE 2:49

IMAGINE YOUNG JESUS, so studious in the Temple (see
Luke 2:41-48). Imagine his mother's horror as she
couldn't find her son in the crowded city. But young Jesus
seems to be completely serious when he asks, "Didn't
you know I'd be here?" If she hadn't been so worried
and distracted, she might have thought of the Temple
sooner—because Jesus was always seeking his Father,
always seeking God's will for his life.

We can follow his example. We can spend all our
time and energy seeking God, looking for him in every
moment of our lives, and keeping in constant touch.

*The determined fixing of our will upon God, and
pressing toward him steadily and without deflection;
this is the very center and the art of prayer.*

EVELYN UNDERHILL

HUNGRY NOW

*God blesses you who are hungry now,
for you will be satisfied.*

LUKE 6:21

ABOUT 13 PERCENT of the people in the world suffer from hunger. There were hungry people in Jesus' time. There are certainly hungry people now. But Jesus has not forgotten any of them. They may hunger now in this broken world, but Jesus promises they will be blessed. And they won't just be fed; they will be blessed to the point of contentment. It's hard to remember in the midst of suffering just how short this life is, but it is short.

Until we leave this earth, we can be Jesus' hands and feet to those who hunger now.

*We thank You for sheltering us from poverty
and starvation. Blessed be the Lord, for
with Him we came and found love, hope
and a new life in a strange country.*

HANNA KHOURI OF LEBANON,

ON BEHALF OF THE REFUGEES FROM PALESTINE

THE GOLDEN RULE

Do to others as you would like them to do to you.

LUKE 6:31

THE GOLDEN RULE. Many of us know it so well that it almost feels like second nature. Except it's not. If we each have only one life to live, then our fleshly, human instinct is to make it the best life possible at everyone else's expense. Jesus turns "survival of the fittest" on its head and says, "This life is not about this life." Instead, Jesus wants us to love others. And a simple way to make sure we are living out his love is to always treat people the way we would want them to treat us.

*May the Cross ever remind us of Thy great
love, for a greater love no man hath given.
This is our supreme example, O God.*

CORETTA SCOTT KING

NOT FAR-FETCHED

Stop the weeping! She isn't dead; she's only asleep.

LUKE 8:52

YOU PROBABLY KNOW the story of elderly Sarah, who laughed at God's promise of her giving birth (see Genesis 18:10-14). Many of God's promises seem downright ridiculous to us, too. And when Jesus promised that a little girl who seemed to be dead wasn't, the weepers gathered in the house laughed at him (see Luke 8:49-55). They didn't understand *how much smarter* Jesus is than we are.

Streets of gold? A new city descending out of heaven? (See Revelation 21.) Sounds crazy, right? But don't laugh! Jesus knows so much more about what's to come than we do. If he says it's possible, it is, no matter how far-fetched it seems to us.

> *When Jesus stood outside the door of the dead little girl's home and told the crowd to stop mourning, their response was to laugh. They knew dead when they saw it. But Jesus saw what they could not.*
>
> SUZANNE ELLER

HEAVEN BOUND

Don't rejoice because evil spirits obey you; rejoice because your names are registered in heaven.

LUKE 10:20

JESUS GAVE HIS DISCIPLES authority over Satan and his demons (see Luke 10:16-19). Heady stuff! So he quickly told them that this authority was not the point. The *point* was that they would join him in heaven one day, and he was sending them out to find others who would make that journey with them.

Sometimes Jesus gives us a big assignment, but if we let it go to our heads, we are doomed. Even if Jesus makes you famous, brilliant, rich, or powerful, none of that really matters. Our job is to live our lives as if we're heaven bound—because we are, and *that's* what really counts.

No matter where you find yourself in life, you're in a season of celebration.

VICKI KUYPER

LOVE IS A VERB

The Samaritan soothed his wounds with
olive oil and wine and bandaged them. Then
he put the man on his own donkey and took
him to an inn, where he took care of him.

LUKE 10:34

IN THE PARABLE of the Good Samaritan, the hero of the story doesn't say, "I feel like I love you, you poor injured soul!" and then keep walking (see Luke 10:30-37). In fact, Jesus doesn't tell us how the Samaritan *felt*, probably because it doesn't matter.

The hero showed the injured man a hands-on kind of love, a love in action. Feeling love is great, but feelings are fleeting. The love of Jesus is not. If we want to really love someone, we've got to do something about it.

His regard for us goes far beyond kind words
and warm feelings; his is a show-and-tell
love, held up for the whole world to see.

LIZ CURTIS HIGGS

GREATER THAN SOLOMON

*The queen of Sheba will stand up against this
generation on judgment day and condemn it,
for she came from a distant land to hear the
wisdom of Solomon. Now someone greater than
Solomon is here—but you refuse to listen.*

LUKE 11:31

SOLOMON ASKED for wisdom, and God gave it to him
(see 1 Kings 3:5-12). Solomon's wisdom was so great,
a queen from a faraway land traveled just to see it for
herself.

We can get in on that same deal, and we don't even
have to cross a desert for it. Jesus says that he is even wiser
than Solomon, and we have access to him and his words
daily. All we have to do is ask (see James 1:5).

*Christ offers us daily assistance, divine opportunities,
and eternal provision. He also extends to us His Word,
which allows us to arch over the world's distorted
mindset to receive the pure wisdom that is from above.*

PATSY CLAIRMONT

OCTOBER 28

REAL LIGHT

*Make sure that the light you think you
have is not actually darkness.*

LUKE 11:35

ARROGANCE IS A NASTY THING, and many of us suffer
from it. We might not be strutting around telling the
world we're the best thing since sliced bread, but we're
probably still trying to do certain things our way instead
of God's way.

You're pretty smart. You've been to school, you've
read books, and you've got the World Wide Web of information at your fingertips. Sometimes it can be tempting
to think you know what you're doing. But we get into
trouble when we think we know better than God. If the
light in us is of our own making, then it's not really light.

*If our hearts are full of our own wretched
"I ams" we will have no ears to hear His
glorious, soul-satisfying "I Am."*

HANNAH WHITALL SMITH

ONE LOST SINNER

There is more joy in heaven over one lost sinner who repents and returns to God than over ninety-nine others who are righteous and haven't strayed away!

LUKE 15:7

SO MANY TIMES, in so many ways, Jesus tells us that *we matter*. If everyone else was falling in line but you ran off to chase a goose, he would go get you and bring you back.

We need to accept this truth for ourselves, but we also need to accept it for others. When we look at someone, no matter what they look like, what they say, or how they act, they still matter to Jesus. He wants to save that person, even if we don't understand why. We don't have to understand. We just have to love.

In God's economy, the thousands are just as important as the few. The few are just as important as the one.

SUZANNE ELLER

WHO ARE WE TRYING TO IMPRESS?

You like to appear righteous in public, but God knows your hearts. What this world honors is detestable in the sight of God.

LUKE 16:15

WHAT DOES THIS world honor? Power over other people. The ability to manage (control) others. Wealth. Shiny toys. Big houses. Popularity. Fame. Sex appeal.

None of these things bring glory to God; therefore, they are detestable to him. Jesus scolded the Pharisees for worrying more about what others thought of them than about what God thought of them. They strutted around impressing others, but they failed entirely to impress their Creator.

Of course we want to appear upright before others, but that shouldn't be our primary goal. Who are we trying to impress, really?

> *Yea, closest closet of my thought*
> *Hath open windows to thine eyes.*

MARY HERBERT

A GREAT CHASM

Besides, there is a great chasm separating us.
No one can cross over to you from here, and
no one can cross over to us from there.

LUKE 16:26

JESUS PAINTS A FAIRLY scary picture of the afterlife (see Luke 16:19-26). At least, it's scary for people who make the wrong choice in the present life. The rich man, in a place of flaming torment, begs for a drop of water. And Abraham tells him there is a gap between them that no one can cross.

Once we reach our eternal destination, it will be too late to change our minds. This is bad news for some, but it should inspire us to share Jesus' love with others right now, before it's too late.

When you die—you die! There are no second chances.
We always hear people say, "Well, you only live
once!" I am here to tell you, you only die once!

LISA MENDENHALL

SOME WON'T BE PERSUADED

*Abraham said, "If they won't listen to Moses
and the prophets, they won't be persuaded
even if someone rises from the dead."*

LUKE 16:31

IF YOU'VE EVER TRIED to share the gospel with someone,
you probably know what rejection feels like. You probably know what it's like to be ignored, mocked, or ridiculed. And this can be painful. It can hurt to be rejected,
and it can hurt us to see Jesus rejected. It can also make
us feel as though we've failed at leading someone to Jesus.

In Jesus' story, Abraham says that some people just
won't listen no matter what. And we can't make them
listen. All we can do is share Jesus' love and let the Holy
Spirit do the rest.

*While God may use you in great ways as an influence,
ultimately it's the Holy Spirit's job to change hearts.*

NANCY KENNEDY

True Rebuke

Watch yourselves! If another believer sins, rebuke that person; then if there is repentance, forgive.

LUKE 17:3

THE WORD *REBUKE* is a scary one. It can bring to mind a stern schoolmarm with a ruler in her hand. But a real rebuke from a brother or sister acting on behalf of God is not a scary thing. It will feel more like a hug than a sting—because someone acting on the urging of the Holy Spirit will speak to you in a loving, gentle, compassionate way.

The Holy Spirit within you will help you to receive that rebuke in the spirit in which it was intended. True rebuke will make you stronger and healthier. That's the way God designed it.

I honestly don't know where I would be today if my friends hadn't loved me enough to point out inappropriate things in me that needed attention.

LUCI SWINDOLL

OUR DUTY

When you obey me you should say, "We are unworthy
servants who have simply done our duty."

LUKE 17:10

WHEN WE WORK hard for Jesus, sometimes people take notice. They might praise us, applaud us, or give us a hearty slap on the back. And it can be tempting to accept these accolades. After all, we've worked hard, right?

But in this verse, Jesus gently tells us not to take a big, self-congratulating bow. Instead, he asks us to remind our admirers why we do what we do—we do it all for *him*. We love others because he first loved us. We serve others because he first served us. Let's give the credit to the one who deserves it, and maybe by doing this, others will look to him.

I am so small;
you are so all.

VERONICA ZUNDEL

DON'T LOOK BACK!

Remember what happened to Lot's wife!

LUKE 17:32

POOR LOT'S WIFE. She was asked to leave her home and told to not even glance back (see Genesis 19:15-26). How many of us would have done as she did and sneaked a quick peek? It's hard to leave things, people, places behind. We grow attached. These things start to feel as though they are part of who we are.

Yet so often Jesus asks us to do just this: to leave parts of our old selves behind. This might mean people we care about, places we've stayed, or activities we've enjoyed. It will most definitely mean sin. Even when sin feels comfortable and safe, it's still sin, and Jesus asks us to walk away from it and not look back.

> *What was she doing, waiting there*
> *with darkness spattering the air;*
> *don't hang your hearts on things, she'd said.*

KAREN GERSHON

NOVEMBER 5

CRY OUT TO HIM
DAY AND NIGHT

*[The judge said,] "This woman is driving me crazy.
I'm going to see that she gets justice, because she
is wearing me out with her constant requests!"*

LUKE 18:5

EVER FEEL AS THOUGH YOU'RE NAGGING JESUS? Jesus told
a parable about an unfair judge who finally gave justice to
a widow who wouldn't leave him alone (see Luke 18:1-7).
If that judge finally did what was right, how much sooner
will our just God?

If we are asking things according to God's will, with
our hearts in the right place, then we need to keep asking
without giving up. Jesus likes to hear from us, often. Day
and night, he hears our prayers.

*Prayer is the portal that brings the power of
heaven down to earth. It is kryptonite to the
enemy and to all his ploys against you.*

PRISCILLA SHIRER

WHEN HE FINDS US

When the Son of Man returns, how many
will he find on the earth who have faith?

LUKE 18:8

WHEN YOU IMAGINE Jesus' return, is your heart filled
with excitement or dread? If you say *dread*, you're not
alone. Many of us feel uneasiness about what Jesus will
find when he suddenly appears. What will we be doing,
thinking, and saying when he shows up? But if we have
this sense of unease, it's a good sign that we need to make
some adjustments.

Jesus may not show up during our lifetime, but each
of us will die at some point, and we may not see it coming. We may not have a lot of time to get ready to meet
Jesus. Let's get our affairs in order now so we'll be ready
when he finds us.

What's my goal? What's my ambition?
Is it my happiness or my holiness?

KAY ARTHUR

THE EYE OF THE NEEDLE

It is easier for a camel to go through the
eye of a needle than for a rich person
to enter the Kingdom of God!

LUKE 18:25

YOU MAY NOT THINK of yourself as rich, but if you've got clothes on your body, food in your pantry, and a roof over your head, you're quite rich in comparison to millions of people in the world. So these words from Jesus are a sober heads-up.

Even if we feel secure in our lives, we still need to recognize that we're really not—not without Jesus. Regardless of the balance in our bank accounts, we need to be always actively seeking him. *That's* the way through the eye of the needle.

Rich man, rich man, who are you?
Do you seek the Christ Child, too? . . .
Can you get your camel through
The needle's eye, as you must do?

ELIZABETH ROONEY

A Donkey?

*Go into that village over there. . . . As you enter
it, you will see a young donkey tied there that no
one has ever ridden. Untie it and bring it here.*

Luke 19:30

Jesus told his disciples to go get a donkey that wasn't
theirs. They were probably bewildered by this command.
First of all, how did Jesus know that there was a donkey there? How did he know it had never been ridden?
Wasn't someone going to mind if the disciples just suddenly snatched a donkey? And finally, what on earth did
Jesus need a donkey for?

This is such a great example of the big picture Jesus
sees and the small, silly questions we often ask as we try
to follow his commands.

*We have to stand in the complexity of all
that God is working on, not just in the
simple part we can see for ourselves.*

NICOLE JOHNSON

QUESTION, THEN LISTEN

*[The priests and leaders] demanded, "By
what authority are you doing all these
things? Who gave you the right?"
"Let me ask you a question first," [Jesus] replied.*

LUKE 20:2-3

THROUGHOUT SCRIPTURE, Jesus answered questions
with questions. For starters, these question-answers kept
him from getting stuck in the traps the religious leaders
set for him. Also, when people tried to answer Jesus' questions, their own faulty reasoning would often be exposed.

But most obviously, when Jesus asked questions, he
was showing that he cared about the people he was ques-
tioning. He didn't just ask a question and then walk away,
or stare straight ahead waiting until it was his turn to
talk again. Jesus was a true listener. We would do well to
follow his example. So the next time someone asks you
a question, try answering with a question of your own.
Then listen.

Listening shows that someone cares.
CATHARINE BRANDT

NO MARRIAGE IN HEAVEN

In the age to come, those worthy of being raised from the dead will neither marry nor be given in marriage.

LUKE 20:35

MARRIAGE WAS DESIGNED to be a beautiful commitment between a husband and wife that gives us an example of Jesus' relationship with his church. Because we live in a broken world, so many marriages are broken, breaking, or suffering. When we get to heaven, we won't need the example of marriage anymore, because we'll be living out the real deal.

If you have been blessed with a healthy marriage, then enjoy it and pray for your sisters who are struggling in their marriages. But if you're working through an unhealthy marriage, don't lose heart. Jesus has so much more in store for you in heaven.

A man can never totally satisfy your craving for love. His humanity will not allow him to.
MICHELLE MCKINNEY HAMMOND

THEY WILL BE LIKE ANGELS

*They will never die again. In this respect
they will be like angels. They are children of
God and children of the resurrection.*

LUKE 20:36

PEOPLE ARE NOT ANGELS. We are entirely different beings. And we don't turn into angels when we die. But Jesus does say we "will be like angels." What a beautiful future these words paint. We will live among the angels as children of God. Each of us will die, but we will be resurrected and then "never die again."

When we understand and believe these words of Jesus, death is not scary. It is certainly sad for the loved ones we leave behind. But think of what we're going *to*. We go to Jesus. We go to paradise. We go to glory. We go home.

I do not wait for the undertaker, but for the Uptaker.

CORRIE TEN BOOM

DON'T LET YOUR HEARTS BE DULLED

*Watch out! Don't let your hearts be
dulled by carousing and drunkenness,
and by the worries of this life.*

LUKE 21:34

JESUS NAMES TWO THINGS that can dull our hearts:
drunkenness and anxiety. Interesting how these two
enemies work together in our world today. Many people
try to solve anxiety with alcohol, or even drugs, and the
resultant lack of judgment often leads to more anxiety. It
makes sense then that Jesus would tell us to watch out!

Anxiety is a fierce beast, especially in a world that
moves as fast as ours. But we don't have to fall prey to
it. Protect your heart: give your worries, your cares, your
fears to Jesus.

*Lord Jesus Christ, our God, the worries and cares
of our lives beat up against us in great waves. Help
us to see Thee walking over the surging waters.*

PRINCESS ILEANA OF ROMANIA

THE NEW COVENANT

*This cup is the new covenant between God and
his people—an agreement confirmed with my
blood, which is poured out as a sacrifice for you.*

LUKE 22:20

AT THE LAST SUPPER, Jesus revealed the heart of God
toward his people. God made a new covenant with
humankind in order to save our lives and bring us into a
relationship with him.

This agreement is not complicated: Jesus poured out
his life for us when he died a horrible sacrificial death. We
believe in him, we accept the gift of his life, and we start
to follow him. That is the new covenant. That is the deal
that gifts you with eternal life, a life that starts the second
you say yes to Jesus.

For nothing good have I
Whereby Thy grace to claim;
I'll wash my garments white
In the blood of Calvary's Lamb.

ELVINA MABLE HALL

SIFTINGS

Simon, Simon, Satan has asked to
sift each of you like wheat.

LUKE 22:31

WHEN JESUS TOLD Simon Peter that Satan had asked to "sift [him] like wheat," Peter probably wasn't thrilled. It certainly wasn't pleasant for Job when God gave Satan permission to test him (see Job 1:12). But this is what happens when we follow Jesus.

When we are steady on the path to growth, joy, and peace, the enemy takes notice and tries to throw us off track. In the short run, this can be incredibly unpleasant. But in the long run, these "siftings" cause us to depend more on Jesus as we push through the fight. The next time God allows Satan to sift you, faithfully trust Jesus to help you persevere.

God allows hardships for divine purposes. Our
faith is increased through each trial, and we learn
to trust God's faithfulness and accept His mercy.

SHARON GLASGOW

STRENGTHEN YOUR SISTERS

*I have pleaded in prayer for you, Simon, that your
faith should not fail. So when you have repented
and turned to me again, strengthen your brothers.*

LUKE 22:32

IN TODAY'S VERSE Jesus presented Simon Peter with
a fairly straightforward plan: (1) I've prayed for you,
(2) repent and get back on track, and (3) strengthen your
brothers.

Peter had gotten off track. We will get off track too.
But thanks to Jesus, we can always get back on. All we
have to do is repent and start following him again. Then
we will be able to help our brothers and sisters. Then
we will be able to love them, strengthen them, and help
them stay on track as well. That's Kingdom living.

*When we, by ourselves, know who we are in Christ,
when we have a strong personal relationship with
Him, then we have so much to offer each other.*

SHEILA WALSH

CLEARLY PREDICTED

Wasn't it clearly predicted that the
Messiah would have to suffer all these
things before entering his glory?

LUKE 24:26

IT ISN'T PLEASANT to think about all the suffering Jesus endured for our sake—even just the overwhelming physical pain of being nailed to an upright cross. But sometimes we need to think about what he was willing to go through because of his love for us.

We can be encouraged by the fact that God put his redemptive plan in motion the second sin entered the world. Jesus *chose* to suffer for us. He knew what he was getting himself into, and he believed that *you* were worth it. Your salvation was worth his suffering. So next time you feel as if you're not loved or you're not good enough or you're not special, think again.

he is not beautiful
blood sweats from him in rain
VERONICA ZUNDEL

JESUS WANTS TO SPEND TIME WITH YOU

Do you have anything here to eat?

LUKE 24:41

AFTER THE RESURRECTION and before the Ascension, Jesus appeared to his disciples. After he assured them that he was the real deal, he asked them, simply, for some food.

Even then, even after he was in his new form, he still wanted to spend time with his brothers and sisters. And he still wants to spend time with us. We may not be able to serve him a piece of broiled fish, but we can sit down with him, talk to him, read his Word, and just hang out with him.

> *Prayer is our being in a constant state of understanding that we are in his presence, talking with him as we would a friend—a father—and being ever intent on hearing his voice as he speaks to us.*

EVA MARIE EVERSON

THE MESSAGE

*It was also written that this message would be
proclaimed in the authority of his name to all
the nations, beginning in Jerusalem: "There
is forgiveness of sins for all who repent."*

LUKE 24:47

HERE IS THE GOSPEL in a nutshell: repent, and your sins
will be forgiven. Jesus shared this message with his disciples, who still didn't fully understand why Jesus had
died and risen again. But they did as Jesus asked. They
spread his Good News from Jerusalem to surrounding
nations.

We have heard Jesus' story, thanks to their efforts.
Now it is up to us to keep spreading the word: there is
forgiveness for all who repent.

*Forgive us for all our sins and mistakes. Throw
them all into the pit of forgetting, because we pray
in the name of Jesus Christ, our Saviour, thy Son.*

BOLUMBU SALA

THE HEART BUSINESS

*Now here is a genuine son of Israel—
a man of complete integrity.*

JOHN 1:47

JESUS WAS CALLING his disciples (see John 1:43-48). He called Philip, who then went to look for Nathanael, telling him, "He's here! The Messiah! We've found him!"

When the two men returned to Jesus, Jesus spoke to Nathanael, calling him "a man of complete integrity." Imagine Nathanael's reaction. He'd never met this man. How could Jesus know anything about his heart?

But that's the business Jesus is in: the heart business. He *does* know our hearts, every nook and cranny, and he doesn't have to see us coming to know what's going on in our souls. He knows your heart. And he loves you anyway.

*Make of me what I wish my children to be,
with a heart that is strong, true and great.*

A MOTHER IN AFRICA

YOU JUST WAIT!

*Do you believe this just because I told you
I had seen you under the fig tree? You
will see greater things than this.*

JOHN 1:50

NATHANAEL WAS IMPRESSED that Jesus could miraculously see him, even when they were not in the same place. But Jesus said, "You think that was great? Watch this!" Remember the day you first started following Jesus? Think of all you have learned about him since that day. Jesus could have said to you when you first met him, "You think this is great? You just wait!"

Every time Jesus impresses us, we haven't even seen a fraction of what he can do. There is so much more he will do in our lives. Are you ready to "see greater things" as you follow Jesus?

*If we can acknowledge that what we see in the world is
not all there is, we are strengthening our eyes of faith.*

NICOLE JOHNSON

HEAVENLY THINGS

If you don't believe me when I tell you about
earthly things, how can you possibly believe
if I tell you about heavenly things?

JOHN 3:12

SOMETIMES WHEN WE'RE seeking God, we ask some
pretty tough questions. We want to understand the *why*
of things. We want to see the big picture. And in these
moments, Jesus could easily say to us, "Do you even
believe the things I've already told you?"

Do we? Really? Have we really accepted everything
he's taught us? Do we believe in all his promises? If no,
then maybe we should focus on believing what he's
already done for us before we ask for more knowledge.
After all, we don't need to know it all in order to believe.

Making sense of God's call is not a prerequisite for
following it. His Word and His promises are enough.

PRISCILLA SHIRER

DARKNESS OR LIGHT?

The judgment is based on this fact: God's light came into the world, but people loved the darkness more than the light, for their actions were evil.

JOHN 3:19

WE DON'T HAVE to guess at God's grounds for judgment. Jesus makes it clear, and the terms are simple. God put his light into the world, but people love darkness. Some people will *choose* the darkness over the light. God knew this when he created us. He gave us free will. We get to choose: light or dark?

We can't make others' choice for them. All we can do is make our own choice, boldly, and then let God's light shine through us.

then break me wide your raging word
in flintstruck light from darkness stirred
and break me wide your dancing love
that sours the hawk, that swoops the dove

VERONICA ZUNDEL

EXPOSED

All who do evil hate the light and refuse to go
near it for fear their sins will be exposed.

JOHN 3:20

MOST CRIMES HAPPEN at night, in the dark. Criminals don't want to get caught, so why would they commit crimes in the light? There is a spiritual truth here: it is unpleasant to face sin. When we acknowledge it, we have to deal with it. It can be embarrassing. It can hurt.

It's much easier to keep on operating in the darkness, because the darkness doesn't challenge us. We're used to it. It might even feel safe. But it's not—because it's darkness. We need to boldly step out into the light, even if it's scary, even if it hurts.

If pain comes as we're freed,
Your daylight must have hurt first Lazarus's eyes.

MADELEINE L'ENGLE

A TEAM EFFORT

You know the saying, "One plants and another harvests." And it's true. I sent you to harvest where you didn't plant; others had already done the work, and now you will get to gather the harvest.

JOHN 4:37-38

SOMETIMES IT SEEMS God surrounds us with people who are hungry for him. Everywhere we turn, someone is coming to Jesus. We had better not think this means we are special! It just means that other people have laid the foundation before we got there.

Likewise, sometimes we'll feel like all we're doing is planting seeds. But don't be discouraged. God has other people lined up to water those seeds!

It is easy to believe that God can use our lives when we see immediate results, when positive feedback encourages us to push on. It is hard to keep walking when we see little sign that what we are doing is making a difference.

SHEILA WALSH

NOW YOU ARE WELL

Now you are well; so stop sinning, or
something even worse may happen to you.

JOHN 5:14

JESUS SPOKE THESE words to a man he'd cured from an illness (see John 5:8-9). His words suggest a link between sin and physical well-being. It's not that everyone who is ill has done something to deserve it, but there is a general principle here: our decisions often affect our health.

They especially affect our spiritual health. If we want to be spiritually well, we need to stop sinning. No one can stop completely, but we can surely claim victory over sin and live as if we have the power of Jesus living within us, because we do.

I was made for more than being stuck in
a vicious cycle of defeat. I am not made
to be a victim of my poor choices. I was
made to be a victorious child of God.

LYSA TERKEURST

THOSE WHO LISTEN
WILL LIVE

I assure you that the time is coming, indeed it's here now, when the dead will hear my voice—the voice of the Son of God. And those who listen will live.

JOHN 5:25

WE HAVE A CHOICE. We can walk around this world like zombies, blindly pursuing our next source of entertainment. We can sprint through this world like rabbits, zigzagging from one task to the next and never getting anywhere. Or we can live peacefully like sisters of the Son of God, like women who have heard the very voice of God and have chosen to let that voice inside our hearts, where it has changed everything, where it has given us life.

Open my ears, that I may hear
Voices of truth Thou soundest clear.
And while the wave notes fall on my ear,
Everything false will disappear.

CLARA H. FISKE SCOTT

IGNORE THE CRITICS

*Your approval means nothing to me, because
I know you don't have God's love within you.*

JOHN 5:41-42

MANY OF US were raised to be "good girls." We enjoyed praise for our good behavior and cringed at criticism and correction, which usually meant we'd done something wrong.

If we are living our lives for Jesus, people will criticize and try to correct us. They will mock us and call us foolish, or worse. They will accuse us of horrible things: living a lie, ruining our children, ruining our country. But they're wrong.

We good girls might miss the affirmations we used to get, but we shouldn't seek them out. We don't need the world's approval. We just need Jesus' approval.

*The degree to which you seek God's approval
over man's acceptance is the degree to
which God can use you mightily.*

CHRISTINE CAINE

THE HONOR THAT MATTERS

*No wonder you can't believe! For you gladly honor
each other, but you don't care about the honor
that comes from the one who alone is God.*

JOHN 5:44

IF A GROUP OF PEOPLE sat down in a circle and each one
began to rub the back of the person to their right, they
would all be feeling pretty good about their little arrangement. But how does Jesus get into the circle? He can't.
How can those in need get help from the circle? They
can't. How does the circle grow? It won't.

It might feel good to be part of a group whose members honor only one another, but that's not how Jesus
wants his people to behave. Jesus wants the circle to grow.

*God's opinion is the only one that matters, and His
pleasure isn't necessarily measured in book sales,
income generated, or pats on the back from others.*

ROBIN CHADDOCK

AN ENERGY AUDIT

*Spend your energy seeking the eternal life
that the Son of Man can give you. For God the
Father has given me the seal of his approval.*

JOHN 6:27

THIS WORLD OFFERS us no shortage of ways to spend our
energy: parenthood, careers, physical pleasures, romance,
art, entertainment, recreation. None of these things are
necessarily bad, but they take our energy in a direction
other than the one Jesus has given us: eternal life.

Jesus tells us to invest our energy where it matters: in
the Kingdom of God. Why spend our energy on things
that have no eternal value when we can invest it in something that will never end? The world won't make it easy,
but Jesus will make it possible.

*Hold on to Christ with your teeth
if your hands get crippled.*
ELIZABETH PRENTISS

THE ONLY WORK GOD WANTS

*This is the only work God wants from
you: Believe in the one he has sent.*

JOHN 6:29

IT'S SO GREAT when Jesus makes it simple for us! It's easy
to be overwhelmed with gratitude for all Jesus has done
for us, and that gratitude often manifests in a desire to
do stuff for God.

Serving is great, but it's not the most important thing.
The most important thing is that we *believe*. Doing good
works won't give us a relationship with Jesus. Belief will.
Doing good deeds won't get us into heaven. Belief will.
Organizing projects and events for church won't give us
a healthy, content life. Belief in Jesus will.

*And faith and hope and love
Will be
The warp and woof
Of fabric gay
That I would weave for thee today.*

UTAKO HAYASHI

ONLY GOOD
STUFF REMAINS

That is why I said that you will die in your sins; for unless you believe that I AM who I claim to be, you will die in your sins.

JOHN 8:24

WHEN IT'S TIME to leave this earth, we may be able to look back on our lives. Wouldn't it be great to re-experience love, joy, peace, and hope as we look back? Wouldn't it be horrible to relive incidents that gave us grief and regret?

We all make mistakes. We all sin. But a relationship with Jesus wipes the slate clean and allows us to look back on our lives and smile, knowing that Jesus has washed away the bad stuff, and only good stuff remains.

We're so occupied with today that we take no thought for our future and eternity—that is, until somehow we're brought face to face with the specter of death.

KAY ARTHUR

THEN YOU WILL UNDERSTAND

When you have lifted up the Son of Man on the cross, then you will understand that I AM he.

JOHN 8:28

THE UNBELIEVERS just didn't get it. They refused to. So Jesus said, "I'll die and come back to life. Then you'll understand." We can hope that they did see, that they did understand, and that they did choose to give their hearts to Jesus.

So many people today just don't get it. They refuse to. They make excuses. They get their impressions of faith from individuals or churches, instead of looking at the only one who matters—Jesus. We can hope that the people around us will look at Jesus, who was lifted up on the cross. That's the only way they will ever understand.

Take a long look at what happened at Calvary. The agony there was of the just for the unjust.

ELISABETH ELLIOT

LIVE IN FREEDOM

I tell you the truth, everyone who sins is a slave of sin.

JOHN 8:34

EVERYONE. Each and every one of us was born a slave to sin. On our own, we are powerless to overcome it. That is why we need Jesus. He will not only forgive us of our sins but also give us the ability to overcome future temptations.

Once we choose Jesus, we no longer have to let sin control our lives. We can choose to live in freedom. We can choose to let the Holy Spirit have control.

> *Living in freedom means learning how to walk again—learning how to walk God's way for a change—because, listen, you can be 100 percent saved and still spend the majority of your time in Egypt. Unbelievers aren't the only ones who contribute to Egypt's overcrowding.*

PRISCILLA SHIRER

ADOPTION IS PERMANENT

A slave is not a permanent member of the
family, but a son is part of the family forever.

JOHN 8:35

WE ARE BORN into this world as slaves to sin. But when
we choose to follow Jesus, we are adopted into God's
family, and that is a forever deal.

Adoption isn't temporary. It's permanent. It can't be
undone. Even death doesn't change it. We will still sin,
because we're still human, but God doesn't abandon us.
He doesn't give up. We are his children, and he will continue to discipline, protect, and love us until he brings
us home.

When we humble ourselves, quit fast-forwarding
past the bad parts, and admit that we're lost
without Him, we become His unlikely children.
Desperate, imperfect people . . . completely adored,
accepted, and beloved by a perfect God.

LISA HARPER

LISTEN!

Why can't you understand what I am saying?
It's because you can't even hear me!

JOHN 8:43

HAVE YOU EVER sat through a class without hearing a word the teacher said? We can stare out the window, stare at our doodles, or stare directly at the instructor so we *look* like we're listening. We do this when we don't really care what the professor is saying or when we're distracted by other things in our lives.

People did this to Jesus. They do it to him now. Even after we've chosen to follow Jesus, we can still tune out the Holy Spirit. But when we do, we will suffer the consequences. We will blow up the lab experiment or fail the quiz, and we'll wish we'd listened.

Let us in the stillness of our hearts pray
that we may have the consciousness of
His presence and listen to His voice.

MICHI KAWAI

WHILE WE STILL CAN

We must quickly carry out the tasks assigned
us by the one who sent us. The night is
coming, and then no one can work.

JOHN 9:4

JESUS SPOKE THESE words to his disciples. It was as if he were saying, "Our time is limited, and we've got lots of work to do."

We are eternal beings, but our time on earth is limited, and there's still a lot to accomplish. When God gives us a task to do, we shouldn't procrastinate. We shouldn't waste time making excuses. We need to get right to work. We need to help others while we can. We need to tell others about Jesus while we can—before it's too late.

Show me the possibility of Thy Gospel in my time, that
I may not give up the daily, hourly battle in its defense.

GABRIELA MISTRAL

CHOOSING TO SEE

*I entered this world to render judgment—
to give sight to the blind and to show those
who think they see that they are blind.*

JOHN 9:39

JESUS CAME TO SHOW the humble the light and to let the proud stay in their own darkness. He doesn't force anyone's eyes open. He leaves it up to us. If we want to see him, Jesus will open our eyes. If we're content in our own blindness, Jesus will let us stay there.

We can't force other people's eyes open either. We can just tell them about the light of Jesus and hope they'll choose to open their hearts to him.

*Lord, open Thou our eyes that we may see our
sins of omission and commission in the light
of the radiant life of Thy only begotten Son.*

SARAH CHAKKO

UNALTERED AND UNALTERABLE

You know that the Scriptures cannot be altered.

JOHN 10:35

NO ONE CAN alter the Word of God. This is such good news! It is nothing short of a miracle that the Bible has survived for so long, that the words penned by people inspired by the Holy Spirit have maintained their integrity for thousands of years, even though people have tried to change them and distort them. God wouldn't allow it.

God won't allow the enemy, or anyone, to add to his Word or take away from it, because it's *his truth*. God has preserved it all these years, and he will continue to do so. That's why we can count on it.

The Bible presents true truth, truth that is unchanging, truth that fits in with what exists, truth that answers the questions of life.

EDITH SCHAEFFER

RESURRECTION POWER

Lazarus, come out!

JOHN 11:43

THE RESURRECTION of Lazarus was one of the final miracles of Jesus' earthly ministry (see John 11:39-44). With many, many people watching, Jesus called a dead man out of the tomb. Lazarus had been in there for *four days*. It's not that Jesus resuscitated him after a few minutes of not breathing. No one could say that Jesus simply woke him from a deep sleep. Lazarus was *dead*. He was in the tomb, wrapped in grave clothes, decomposing. But it didn't matter to Jesus because his resurrection power is unlimited.

Jesus brought Lazarus out of the tomb. He rescued him from death. And he will rescue us from death too. He will give us a new life. All we have to do is believe that he can.

Jesus holds resurrection power—do we hold belief?

RACHEL OLSEN

앗

GRAVECLOTHES

Unwrap him and let him go!
JOHN 11:44

JESUS BROUGHT Lazarus back from the dead, but Lazarus was still wearing his graveclothes (see John 11:39-44). His hands and feet were still bound. He was alive, but he wasn't able to do any real living unless he got some further assistance. Jesus didn't unwrap him. He told the people standing nearby to do it.

Jesus saves us from spiritual death. But that's not the end of the story. Most of us come back to life still bound in graveclothes. We've got baggage. We've got issues. And usually, Jesus doesn't take them off for us instantly. He allows other believers to help us.

Letting our brothers and sisters disciple us is so important. And so is discipling new believers. We have to help them out of their graveclothes.

O come, dear Lord, unbind: like Lazarus, I lie wrapped in stifling grave clothes of self-will.
MADELEINE L'ENGLE

THE WINNING SIDE

*The time for judging this world has come, when
Satan, the ruler of this world, will be cast out.*

JOHN 12:31

IF YOU'VE EVER READ or watched a thriller, you know
how nail-biting the last few minutes can be. You probably know, on some level, that the hero will win, but just
getting to that triumphant resolution can be stressful.

We are watching Jesus' story play out. It can be a bit
stressful. But Jesus has already won this war. He won
it on the cross. Satan can cause us much grief, but his
power is limited. His time is limited. He's already lost.
We shouldn't give him more credit than he is due. We
want to be on the winning side at the end of the story.

*It is foolish to underestimate the power of
Satan, but it is fatal to overestimate it.*

CORRIE TEN BOOM

HIS

Unless I wash you, you won't belong to me.

JOHN 13:8

WE CAN UNDERSTAND why Peter balked at the idea of Jesus washing his feet (see John 13:6-8). But Jesus answered him with a bit of prophetic poetry: "Unless I wash you, you won't belong to me."

We can't belong to Jesus unless we allow his blood to wash away our sins. We can't come to Jesus without repenting, without giving up our sins. If we are unwilling to let go of our sins and receive his forgiveness, then he wants no part of us. What good would we be to him if we stayed dead? He wants to transform us into living, breathing, thriving sisters. Then, and only then, are we his.

Blessed assurance, Jesus is mine!
O what a foretaste of glory divine!
Heir of salvation, purchase of God,
Born of His Spirit, washed in His blood.

FANNY J. CROSBY

ASK IN HIS NAME

You can ask for anything in my name, and I will do it, so that the Son can bring glory to the Father.

JOHN 14:13

THIS IS ONE of Jesus' sweetest promises: if we ask for something in his name, he will do it. Most of us have seen this play out in our lives, but if you haven't, keep praying, because it will happen.

Jesus doesn't make false promises. When we pray continually (see 1 Thessalonians 5:17) according to the will of God (see 1 John 5:14), believe that God will do what we are asking (see Mark 11:24), and ask it in Jesus' name, *he will do it.*

Jesus answers prayer, not to glorify you, not to glorify himself, but to bring glory to God the Father, the Creator of the universe.

Lord, please do this . . . or do something better!

PRISCILLA SHIRER

HE PRAYED FOR YOU

I am praying not only for these disciples but also for all who will ever believe in me through their message.

JOHN 17:20

BEFORE JESUS went to the Cross, he knelt in the garden of Gethsemane and prayed—*for you*. It's hard not to feel loved, not to feel special, and not to feel wanted when we meditate on this fact.

We are those people who believe in Jesus because of the gospel message the disciples worked, suffered, and, in many cases, died to spread. We were always part of Jesus' plan, and he still welcomes newcomers. If someone starts to follow Jesus today, he will welcome them with open arms and say, "I prayed for you."

Prayers from our lonely, troubled lips mix with the prayers of the risen Christ on our behalf.

BONNIE KEEN

LINKED IN FAITH

*I pray that they will all be one, just as you
and I are one—as you are in me, Father,
and I am in you. And may they be in us so
that the world will believe you sent me.*

JOHN 17:21

OFTEN, IT IS SIMPLE fear that prevents believers from living in unity. What is different can frighten us, and when we are fearful, we don't reach out in love. We build walls that separate us from our brothers and sisters. We make excuses that prevent us from getting to know them. And how can we love them if we never get to know them?

Jesus prayed for our unity. Let's not let fear get in the way.

*May the love of Christ within us truly cast
out all fear of one another and make of us
one community linked in faith with God.*

ELSE NIEMOELLER

TRUE TRUTH

*I was born and came into the world to
testify to the truth. All who love the truth
recognize that what I say is true.*

JOHN 18:37

TRUTH. There are people today who say there is no such
thing, that our perceptions establish what is true for us.
This might have a nice philosophical ring to it, but God is
always true, whether or not someone perceives that he is.

Jesus was truly born, he truly grew up, he truly traveled around healing real people, he truly died, and he
truly rose from the grave to testify to that truth. There's
a lot of foolishness in the world to get bogged down in,
but we believers can always cling to God's Word, which
is true, always.

*I need truth in strong doses like a great
cup of coffee in the morning.*

NICOLE JOHNSON

MIND YOUR OWN BUSINESS

If I want him to remain alive until I return,
what is that to you? As for you, follow me.

JOHN 21:22

THIS VERSE IS Jesus' polite way of saying, "Mind your own business." He had just told Peter that he would suffer in the future (see John 21:18-21). And Peter, understandably, says, "What about John? Won't he have to suffer too?" It's like the child who says, "Why do I have to go to bed? She's not!"

Jesus says, "Don't worry about John. You just worry about following me."

If we live our lives worrying about other followers, we won't be able to focus on our own relationship with Jesus. We're not in a competition with the next guy. We just need to follow Jesus.

There is no need for comparison. Be happy with
yourself and find satisfaction in your work.

LAILAH GIFTY AKITA

DATES AND TIMES

The Father alone has the authority to set those dates and times, and they are not for you to know.

ACTS 1:7

THOSE POOR DISCIPLES. Before Jesus arrived, they had been expecting a warrior Messiah who was going to restore Israel's kingdom. They weren't expecting a humble man who washed feet and rode donkeys. So just as he was about to ascend to heaven, they asked, "Now are you going to do it? *Now* are you going to fix everything?" (see Acts 1:6).

If we're honest, we've probably asked Jesus similar questions. *Now* can I have a new job? *Now* can I start a new ministry? *Now* can you bless me?

Jesus told his disciples to be patient. We, too, need to be patient, trusting that God knows more about perfect timing than we do.

You and I are living right this minute on a tiny dot of time within a vast sea of God-moments.

PRISCILLA SHIRER

MY CHOSEN INSTRUMENT

*Saul is my chosen instrument to take
my message to the Gentiles and to kings,
as well as to the people of Israel.*

ACTS 9:15

FROM OUR HUMAN standpoint, Paul (Saul) seems like an unlikely apostle candidate (see Acts 9:1). The self-righteous, bullheaded man was out hunting Christians, but God looked down through time and said, "That one. I'm going to use him." What a wise choice it was! Paul was God's "chosen instrument" for a reason. He was up to the task, and he did it well. The Christian landscape would be vastly different without the work of Paul.

God may have called you to do something. You might think you're an unlikely candidate. But God knows what he's doing, and if he says you're his chosen instrument, then you're perfect for the job.

*Every time Saul crucified Christians . . . God
saw Paul preaching the crucified Christ.*

SAMANTHA REED

DON'T FIGHT GOD!

It is useless for you to fight against my will.

ACTS 26:14

BEFORE HIS CONVERSION, Paul was fighting against God—until Jesus appeared and rebuked him (see Acts 26:9-15). Why fight when you know you're up against *God*? But we do it all the time, don't we? God asks us to do something. We say no. God asks us to *stop* doing something. We say no thank you. Like strong-willed children, we kick against his will, which doesn't do *anything* to God, and we end up with sore legs.

If we stopped being stubborn and just said, "Yes, God. You're God, so I'll do what you say," wouldn't we be better off?

> *"O dreary life," we cry, "O dreary life!"*
> *And still the generations of the birds*
> *Sing through our sighing, and the flocks and herds*
> *Serenely live while we are keeping strife*
> *With Heaven's true purpose in us, as a knife*
> *Against which we may struggle!*

ELIZABETH BARRETT BROWNING

EVERY TRIBE AND NATION

*I am sending you to the Gentiles to open their
eyes, so they may turn from darkness to light
and from the power of Satan to God. Then
they will receive forgiveness for their sins and
be given a place among God's people.*

ACTS 26:17-18

IN ACTS, JESUS' FOLLOWERS take the gospel far beyond
the Jewish people into the surrounding nations. The
apostles shared the gospel with everyone, regardless of
nationality, occupation, or gender.

The gospel does not discriminate. *We* have been
welcomed by the gospel, and we should welcome others
with it.

*Our God and our Father, we praise Thee for
Thy Kingdom in Heaven and earth. We thank
Thee it embraces Jew and Gentile, slave and
free, man and woman. We glorify Thee for the
sure hope that one day Thy children from every
nation and tribe and people and tongue shall
stand before Thy throne and see Thy face.*

MARIE HUBBEL

THE MASTER KEYS

I am the living one. I died, but look—I
am alive forever and ever! And I hold
the keys of death and the grave.

REVELATION 1:18

JESUS HOLDS THE KEYS to your grave. He is alive, forever and ever, and he is inviting you to join him in eternity.

If you want to live forever, you must give him permission to unlock your death. There is no way to pick this lock. There are no other keys that will fit. Jesus is the only option. Jesus is the only thing in this life that sets us free—free from sin, free from loneliness, free from hopelessness, and free from death.

Open my eyes, that I may see
Glimpses of truth Thou hast for me;
Place in my hands the wonderful key
That shall unclasp and set me free.

CLARA H. FISKE SCOTT

NO SECOND DEATH

*Anyone with ears to hear must listen to the
Spirit and understand what he is saying
to the churches. Whoever is victorious will
not be harmed by the second death.*

REVELATION 2:11

IF YOU'VE EVER watched a loved one pass from this life
to the next, you know what a moving experience it can
be. There are stories of people who suddenly reach their
arms out to someone no one else can see, or breathe their
last breath with a smile on their face, or seem perfectly
content to make the journey.

This is what awaits those who believe in Jesus. The
first death is only a doorway, and there is no second death
for us.

*Thy children ask Thee . . . to remove all shadow
of doubt from our minds as regards the life
that awaiteth each one of us when we too
shall pass through the gates called death.*

E. T. CAWDRY

HOLY BODIES

I have a few complaints against you. You tolerate some among you whose teaching is like that of Balaam, who showed Balak how to trip up the people of Israel. He taught them to sin by eating food offered to idols and by committing sexual sin.

REVELATION 2:14

BALAAM (a wicked Old Testament prophet) helped Balak (an Old Testament king) entice the Israelites into sexual sin. In the culture of the time, sexual sin was tightly intertwined with idolatry.

It's not so different today, when so much of our society idolizes sexuality itself. Our culture may act as if sexual sin is no big deal, but it always is. Our bodies are temples, and we need to treat them as if they are holy.

Our conduct has a direct influence on how people think about the gospel. The world doesn't judge us by our theology; the world judges us by our behavior.

CAROLYN MAHANEY

ھوھھی DECEMBER 25 *صوھھی*

A NEW NAME

I will give to each one a white stone, and on the stone will be engraved a new name that no one understands except the one who receives it.

REVELATION 2:17

YOUR PARENTS PROBABLY gave you your first name. Jesus knows you better than your parents know you. Your friends may have nicknamed you. Jesus knows you better than your friends do. Maybe you've picked out your own name. Jesus knows you better than *you* know you.

Jesus knows you so well that he has picked out a perfect name for you. When you hear it, you are going to think, "That *is* the perfect name for me."

O Time, the fatal wrack of mortal things,
That draws oblivion's curtains over kings . . .
But he whose name is graved in the white stone
Shall last and shine when all of these are gone.

ANNE BRADSTREET

JESUS HAS BIG PLANS FOR YOU

To all who are victorious, who obey me to the very end, to them I will give authority over all the nations.

REVELATION 2:26

MANY OF US WOULDN'T even *want* authority over nations, but we can readily admit that Jesus is training us for *something*. We don't necessarily know what it is, but Jesus has future plans for all of us.

If you've been a believer for any length of time, you can probably look back in amazement at how you've grown and changed. Jesus is preparing us, molding us, and loving us into these roles he has in store. It won't do any good to argue with him, so we might as well look forward to a future where he will use us mightily.

In God's plan, you've got a part to play. If you know it and believe it, you'll live it.

LYSA TERKEURST

FRESH, BUBBLING SPRING

*Those who drink the water I give will never
be thirsty again. It becomes a fresh, bubbling
spring within them, giving them eternal life.*

JOHN 4:14

JESUS OFFERED living water, which is the Holy Spirit
(see John 7:39). If you have the Holy Spirit living inside
you, you already know this truth. He changes everything.
He is like a bubbling spring coming up out of the deepest part of you, and he gives you renewed life, energy,
courage, love for God, love for others, love for yourself,
joy, peace, patience, gentleness, and self-control (see
Galatians 5:22-23).

This spring within you will give you eternal life—life
that starts the moment you let the living water in.

*Burn God's words into your heart, His thoughts
into your mind and His ways into your
actions; and you'll have a Spirit-filled life.*

ALISA HOPE WAGNER

NO LUKEWARM FAITH

I know all the things you do, that you are neither
hot nor cold. I wish that you were one or the other!
But since you are like lukewarm water, neither
hot nor cold, I will spit you out of my mouth!

REVELATION 3:15-16

YOU MAY LIKE hot coffee and you may like iced coffee, but you probably don't like lukewarm coffee. Jesus wants us to be zealous in our faith, to be alive with the fire of the Holy Spirit. And apparently, Jesus would prefer cold to tepid—because indifference or ambivalence is insulting to Jesus. He died for us! We should at *least* be hot in our faith. If we can't care enough to actively live for Jesus, then we might as well be cold.

Where apathy and indifference have taken
possession, convince, revive and guide,
O Lord, strengthen Thy people!

JORGELINA LOZADA

WHERE DO THE GIFTS COME FROM?

You say, "I am rich. I have everything
I want. I don't need a thing!" And you don't
realize that you are wretched and miserable
and poor and blind and naked.

REVELATION 3:17

IT CAN FEEL GOOD to be self-sufficient. It can feel good
to look around your life and think, "I built this. Nicely
done, self."

It's good to be content, but we need to be content
in *Jesus*, not in our own power, because we didn't really
build any of this. *Everything* we have is a gift. And if we
think we're doing things on our own power, then we are
denying our own wretchedness, our own blindness.

Contentment comes as we . . . trust that what [God]
provides in the midst of our lack is really all we need.

LYDIA BROWNBACK

GOLD

I advise you to buy gold from me—gold that has
been purified by fire. Then you will be rich.

REVELATION 3:18

THE WAY WE "BUY" the gold that Jesus offers is we trade
for it. We can trade in our own will for his gold. We can
trade our sins and our pride. We can hold up our lives
and say, "Take this, Jesus, and give me instead your gold.
I want to be rich in you."

Any other kind of wealth is only an illusion. Any
other kind of wealth dies when we do. If we don't go to
spend eternity with Jesus, we will become poor at death,
no matter what we leave behind.

Our God is the Divine Alchemist. He can take junk
from the rubbish heap of life, and melting this base
refuse in the pure fire of His love, hand us back—gold.

CATHERINE MARSHALL

A BLESSING FOR
REVELATION READERS

*Blessed are those who obey the words
of prophecy written in this book.*

REVELATION 22:7

MOST PEOPLE FIND the study of the book of Revelation
challenging, and some people avoid reading it altogether.
It's a complicated book, for sure, and it can be overwhelming. It can even be frightening. But Jesus promises
a blessing for those who obey the prophecy in this book.

But we can't obey it if we don't read it, hear it, study
it, and by the power of the Holy Spirit, try to understand
it. We probably won't understand all of it during this life,
but we can certainly obey the parts we do understand.

*When you know what God says, what He means,
and how to put His truths into practice, you will
be equipped for every circumstance of life.*

KAY ARTHUR

Do-able. Daily. Devotions.

START ANY DAY THE ONE YEAR WAY.

For Women

The One Year®
Home and
Garden
Devotions

The One Year®
Devotions
for Women

The One Year®
Daily Acts
of Kindness
Devotional

The One Year®
Women of
the Bible

The One Year®
Coffee with
God

The One Year®
Devotional
of Joy and
Laughter

The One Year®
Women's
Friendship
Devotional

The One Year®
Wisdom
for Women
Devotional

The One
Year® Daily
Moments of
Peace

The One Year®
Women in
Christian
History
Devotional

For Men

The One Year® Impact for Living for Men

The One Year® Devotions for Men

The One Year® Father-Daughter Devotions

For Families

The One Year® Family Devotions, Vol. 1

The One Year® Dinner Table Devotions

For Couples

The One Year® Devotions for Couples

The One Year® Love Language Minute Devotional

The One Year® Love Talk Devotional

For Teens

The One Year® Devos for Teens

The One Year® Be-Tween You and God

For Personal Growth

The One Year® at His Feet Devotional

The One Year® Uncommon Life Daily Challenge

The One Year® Recovery Prayer Devotional

The One Year® Book of Amish Peace

The One Year® Experiencing God's Love Devotional

For Bible Study

The One Year® Praying through the Bible

The One Year® Praying the Promises of God

The One Year® Through the Bible Devotional

The One Year® Book of Bible Promises

The One Year® Unlocking the Bible Devotional

CP1377